Mary
for
Today

Mary
for
Today

by
Patricia
Noone
S.C.

THE THOMAS MORE PRESS
Chicago, Illinois

ISBN 0-88347-078-0

I am grateful to the publishers for permission to quote from the following works:

G. P. Putnam's Sons, for The Way of All Women by M. Esther Harding, copyright © 1970 by The C. G. Jung Foundation for Analytical Psychology, Inc.; Knowing Woman by Irene Claremont de Castillejo, copyright © 1973 by the Jung Foundation; The Wise Old Woman by Rix Weaver, copyright © 1973 by the Jung Foundation.

Houghton Mifflin Company, for Mont-St.-Michel and Chartres by Henry Adams, copyright © 1933 by Charles Francis Adams; "Consorting with Angels" and "For the Year of the Insane" from Live or Die by Anne Sexton, copyright © 1966 by Anne Sexton; "The Rowing Endeth" from The Awful Rowing Toward God by Anne Sexton, copyright © 1975 by Loring Conant, Jr.

Oxford University Press, for The Sermons and Devotional Writings of Gerard Manley Hopkins, edited by Christopher Devlin, copyright © 1959 by the Society of Jesus; "The Blessed Mother Compared to the Air We Breathe" from The Poems of Gerard Manley Hopkins, copyright © 1967 by the Society of Jesus.

Doubleday & Company, Inc., for excerpts from The Jerusalem Bible, copyright © 1966 by Darton, Longman & Todd, Ltd. and Doubleday & Company, Inc.; The Mother of Jesus in the New Testament by John McHugh, copyright © 1975 by John McHugh.

The Catholic University of America Press, for Tertullian: Disciplinary, Moral and Ascetical Works, trans. Edwin A. Quain, copyright © 1959 by Fathers of the Church, Inc.; Saint Ambrose: Theological and Dogmatic Works, trans. Roy J. Deferrari, copyright © 1963 by Catholic University of America Press.

Contents

Preface

The ideas *in* this book are personal and deeply felt. The idea *for* this book was not mine.

I may not be the last person I would ask to write on the Blessed Virgin, but I am far from the top of my list. I teach literature, not theology; my formal theological education was pre-Vatican II; I am not sure I would be able to say the rosary all the way through anymore without stumbling. Mary has not been on my mind of late.

But women have, and so has the Church. So in another way she was in my mind without my knowing it, and after the first month or two of research among the experts I found myself answering back here and there out of my own head, shading things differently, frowning at some assumptions which seemed gratuitous, groaning at some of the language, finding myself on the whole more orthodox than I had expected—if one uses as a touchstone of orthodoxy the living Church of today, the vitality of modern Scripture scholarship, the care and concern that so many are pouring into the renewal of our faith.

Karl Rahner remarked after the Council that Catholic theology could be called mature when it had produced as many books on atheism as it had on Mary. I would call that not maturity, but remedial work; real development will come when we are able to tackle the two subjects together, not separately, and when we have brought female atheists into the dialogue as well.

In the meantime, we live with our own questions, and ways of putting together old beliefs and new experience. It is not only of interest, I think, but essential to the quality of our faith life, that we share even provisional solutions and personal stands which are certainly vulnerable to refinement and revision in time. If I seem to speak primarily to and for women, it is not that I think this a subject which concerns them alone, nor are male readers unwelcome. But right now in our history, women have the greater need to come to grips with Mary and the feminine principle she has been made to embody.

Our age has not yet "called her blessed" from the bottom of its heart—that is, with all the resources in human knowledge and experience that belong to us. We can, of course, lay aside form criticism, existentialism, Jungian psychology, and the other facts of life in the twentieth century, and borrow the blessing of an earlier time. But the universal intuition of Marian folklore is that she prefers us to bring what we have—even if it be so unlikely a gift as a juggling act.

I thank all those who have been "helpmates" to me along the way, especially my own sister, the four remarkable women with whom I live, and the publishers of the Thomas More Association, who made me think twice about saying no to their enlightened idea.

Introduction

Does Mary have anything to say to post-Vatican II Christianity?

There are still, clearly, numbers of people who feel that she does—still the stream of visitors to Lourdes, Fatima crusades, parish Rosary Societies, Mariological conventions and seminars and papers; her friends still troop up to light candles at her altar before, during and after the Eucharistic liturgy. There are others who, if they were to speak honestly, would have to say no—who associate her with a cheap and sentimental piety, with a religion rooted in passivity and acceptance of the *status quo*, with a childish morality based on magic and manipulation of the Godhead rather than human acceptance of responsibility for one's actions.

And there are those caught in between, who perceive the basic sanity of the treatment of Mary in the Vatican Council's Constitution on the Church, as a model of faith in hearing and cooperating with the word of God; accepting this as a main thrust, they also affirm the same document's position that forms of Marian piety legitimately vary with diversities of time and culture.[1]

But intellectual assent to both these conciliar teachings still leaves a void, or at least a question: What are

11

the forms of Marian piety appropriate to late 20th century Catholicism?

The question has been compounded since the Council for those women who have grown into a new sense of their own Christian womanhood, and of the need to re-express the basic symbols and doctrines of the faith in terms commensurate with this growth. These women—we, I—have developed the painful habit of laying Church documents and rhetoric against the actual conditions of women, and reading, at times, a contradictory message. It is no wonder, when the question of Mary arises, if we look at her through eyes narrowed with suspicion: Is she really there *for us,* or is she something of a Trojan horse, raised to ambush our aspirations for personhood, human dignity and active co-responsibility for Church and world? Can we relate to her in herself, or has she been so hopelessly idealized into a plaster statue by male projections that the real woman is unreclaimable? Is there any point in trying to reclaim her, or should we not save our energies and work to establish a more fundamentally balanced image of God—for, after all, the true nature of transcendent being as both Mother and Father, male and female or neither, is *the* basic understanding for lack of which, perhaps, Mary has been compensating all this time.

It seems as if starting "at the top" would be the logical way to do it. But others have spoken to this subject provocatively and well.[2] And starting on the human level has its own kind of wisdom, for both subject and method. As far as the subject is concerned,

Mary touches women in vital, sensitive areas of our lives; human concepts of her as an ideal have shaped many of the expectations placed on us, by ourselves and by others, through the centuries. Just as coming to terms with their own mother has been a more painful and crucial task for many women than relating to any patriarchal figure, human or divine, so it is possible that coming to terms with Mary is a task of immediate importance, not a nicety to be attended to after we have straightened out our ideas about transcendent being. Starting "at the bottom," in fact, may involve us in new ways of looking at transcendence, as well as at ourselves.

In terms of methodology, this kind of approach means listening closely to human beings, especially women, as they try to articulate their experience of life. It means facing honestly the failure, the gap, the lack of feeling, in some cases, between us and Mary, and trying not to fix blame, but to understand the fears and doubts. At a time when we speak incessantly of the need for role models and positive attitudes toward the feminine, when all the Christian churches are being called to re-examine existing patterns of access to genuine ministerial service, when even Pope Paul paints Mary as a "liberated woman," why do we hesitate within ourselves? Is it not, clearly, what Caryll Houselander sensed more than thirty years ago, that we cannot imagine her doing anything that we might do, because we cannot imagine her doing anything at all? Christ seems more human to us; the Gospels at least show him angry, frustrated, in tears. She moves like a pale ghost through the background of the Scripture, as so many women move like pale ghosts through the margins of history books, with a patient, passive, unreal kind of virtue.

How hard it is even to conceive of Mary as an individual. Church tradition has presented her as so utterly related that we know nothing of her personal past, her parentage, her social or economic background, nothing of what brought her to the *kairos* of conceiving that she could conceive God and bring him down to earth, hardly anything of her personality or her thoughts and feelings. We deduce that she might have been a rather silent person only because the Evangelists do not quote many of her words. Doctrinally we give the impression, to others if not to ourselves, that the divine had interfered more than customarily with the shaping of her personality from the start, and that she was so perfectly its tool, at least from the moment of her Fiat on, that she had no self to speak of, no ego at all. At best, spiritual writers concede her womanhood, that most invisible and manipulable of concepts.

Contemporary women seek a sense of self, distinct from their roles of wife, mother, housekeeper, nurse (or doctor, athlete, train conductor, anthropologist!). They feel the need to establish a strong and realistic self-concept, a wholeness of body, mind and heart, out of which they can share their gifts and contribute to society. Mary may have had such a self-concept, but it takes an active imagination to discern it through the language and ethos of self-sacrifice which have surrounded her. We fear the loss of self connected with her, perhaps, more than the dangers of emotionalism or status quo religion mentioned earlier. A little honest emotion might be a dynamic force in the Church today, while women without a sense of self are far more likely to derive their security from, and work to maintain, the status quo.

Mary has come to us, we know, through male hearts and minds, with more than a little of the coloration of an anima projection. That is, in Jungian terms, she has become an archetypal figure through which men have personified the positive psychological tendencies of the feminine principle as they conceive of it. She is the embodiment of human tenderness, compassion, nurturance, self-forgetting service to others. But even if we try to work back beyond the idealization to which she was subjected, the difficulty remains: Is she not, ultimately, unknowable to us now? Will we strip away one set of projections only to replace them with another, more modern, perhaps, tailored to a feminist ideal, more comfortable for us than related to the original reality?

This question plagued me as I searched for a starting point. Talking with students of Scripture only confirmed my puzzlement at the freedom with which most people speak of this virtually unknown Nazarene woman. To examine her symbolic function, her role as a force in the history of Christian culture, seemed easy to me; I could deal—and do, in *Chapter Three*—with the dynamic of her myth, on the basis of numerous, well-documented studies of human re-

sponse to her cult, of what we have revealed about
ourselves in the praises we have offered her. But to
have started and ended there would have meant
coming back to my feminist friends with empty hands.
It is not idle curiosity that leads us to urge each
woman to speak her own personal truth, so that we
may know her self as she defines it: we have come to
realize the oppression involved in living up to ideals
imposed by others, the distortions of woman's history
as told by men, the damage done to any woman in
treating her primarily as a symbol rather than as a person. *Chapter Three* might be easier to write, but I
could not allow it to stand by itself, even if the only
thing printed in *Chapters One* and *Two* were question
marks.

The situation, as it turned out, was not quite that
drastic. Four different ways of trying to know Mary as
a person opened up, each with its own difficulties, but
each too with its challenge: studying and praying
over the Gospel (with its sparse direct references to
her, to be sure, but also with the abundant testimony
to be derived from the person and deeds of her son);
drawing deductions from what we know of Jewish
women of her time; studying the traditional dogmatic
teachings of the Church as it realized the implications
of its creed; looking at her through the tricky prism of
popular culture and devotion. I have tried to allow
these methods to meet and illuminate one another.
Cautious respect for each of them seemed important
to me, and I look with joy and anticipation to the
theologians, Scripture scholars and historians who are

pursuing them in depth. The debts I already owe in this regard are apparent in my footnotes.

But this book has a different nature. It is conscious, on the one hand, of the scholars and theologians; on the other, of the women who are not likely to read what they write, who do not, very often, care what they write, who are searching in far other places for the meaning of their womanhood, for whom, in some cases, the Catholic Church would be the last place they would think of seeking help.

I do not suggest that this work is an answer to their questions. I hope it will be apparent, however, that their questions are taken seriously. Nor do I want to overlook the fact that these questions are also being taken seriously by a growing number of feminist-oriented theologians, philosophers and psychologists—the specialists themselves are beginning to close the gap between learning and life. But radical feminists and Christian intellectuals are not the only interested parties to the subject of this book. In my frame of reference, the group of women with serious questions about God and religion is a wider sisterhood (though, granted, one that isn't exactly convinced it *is* a sisterhood)—that is, a group which includes suburban housewives and blue-collar working women, the highly-educated and the high school dropout, the "new" nun and "lay" woman and the alienated "old-Church" Catholic who kneels resignedly through the renewed liturgy with her rosary in her hands. *And* all those women in between.

This highly disparate group has two things in common: they are women, and they live now. Beyond that, generalizations proceed at their own risk.

I suppose we will not be grouped by sex or historical age in the world to come—and yet it seems as if those two root facts must have some kind of meaning in the afterlife, so deeply do they stamp our otherwise stubbornly-held individual identities even now. "In Christ there is neither male nor female" is a text that needs more explanation than it usually gets. In a context of competition and relative worth, it makes a good deal of sense: down with chauvinism, and love your neighbor as yourself. But the lid doesn't quite fit on the box, the note doesn't ring out precisely with bell-like clarity. Are sexual differences a temporary thing, designed to self-destruct after completing the task of providing people for the kingdom? Who are we, male or female, and what are we for, in the end? Should we start practicing for the great androgynous society-in-the-sky, and if so, by which of the many available game plans?

We live now. We cannot wait for the end result of this promising experiment, or that missing piece of information. We *are* the experiment, in our choices and our interaction. We may tinker with theories, but we cannot tinker with people. If womanhood is a gift with any meaning to it, it is not theory but real people, who are women, who must tell us so. Connections must be made. At the risk of a good deal of superficiality and over-simplification, I have tried to make them.

I write primarily in the context of Western culture,

and of women of the First World, though conscious of the vastly different situation and priorities of Third World women—to which group Mary herself belonged. There is urgent need for dialogue between the two groups, as the meetings of the International Women's Year demonstrated; for such dialogue to be fruitful, each side must clarify its vision and goals. "Sisterhood" ought not to be expected to achieve a miracle of instant unity and comprehension when brotherhood among the same nations has worked to such poor effect for so much longer a time.

American women today find themselves called to new roles, which demand for their fulfillment a new vision of the feminine and its capacities. Vast changes in our country's social and economic structure have precipitated changes in the responsibilities traditionally assigned to woman; meeting these responsibilities has in turn opened her eyes to further unmet needs and other areas crying out for her gifts. She looks at a world politically, economically, technologically more complex than her mother could have dreamed of, and foresees the world her children will face, where present complexities are doubled and redoubled—if not first erased by nuclear holocaust. She has not so much chosen the new as she has had it thrust upon her.

Thus she experiences both a sense of dislocation from the past and an acute awareness of its inadequacy to her present situation. She may or may not rejoice in the newness the present contains, but she cannot credit any group or institution which fails to recognize its reality. "I'm convinced," says Anna Wulf in *The Golden Notebook,* "that there are whole areas of me made by the kind of experience women haven't had before . . . I don't want to be told when I wake up, terrified by a dream of total annihilation, because of the H-bomb exploding, that people felt that way about the cross-bow. It isn't true. There is something new in the world."[3]

Newness has its perils for the modern woman. Few institutions or groups have kept pace with it. She is thrown back upon her own strengths, and weaknesses. A religion which does not perceive what has happened to her, which simply calls up old cliches about femininity to address her hopes and fears, will be justly ignored by her.

And yet she desperately needs to believe in her relationship with the divine, to see herself as a direct recipient of the personal love of God, to know in her bones that her life moves toward a transcendent being, and that her own particular being exercises a share in that transcendence. She—we—need to believe that our God and our religion believe in *us,* and endorse our womanhood; and to believe, too, that our womanhood is not a closed and finalized category, but that God and religion are open to the new meanings that we may discover in it. Which is to say, simply, we need a Christianity renewed beyond its present state.

Again, the modern woman feels and speaks of her need for role models—for human company along the way, in the form of women who have succeeded in being true to themselves and active participants in their world. "Role model" is perhaps a poor term. There may be few models for the role she has chosen; few women who were able to choose any role as freely as she to begin with. Even if imitation of past patterns appeared desirable to her, she could not really maintain it. In fact, on very dark days it seems to her that she has not so much been engendered by the generation before hers as she has been shot out of a cannon a great distance off. And though on brighter days she finds the trajectory exhilarating, at no time does it seem to her reversible.

She is wary of role models fetched up out of the past for her by others, and wary too of her own inner temptations of weariness, compliance, nostalgia. For support she looks mostly to her companions in the present, to those who travel the trajectory side by side with her, or perhaps a day or year ahead. Still, she cannot resist looking back, and wanting the longer connection, the roots.

She wonders if those who have gone before her have any strength or energy to give her now, any insight to offer into her sex and her place in history. If she looks closely enough, she may realize that her experience is not absolutely new, but in its own way a development of the aspirations of earlier women who were largely unknown to her. She may find that her impression of disconnectedness has come not only from the speed and magnitude of cultural change, but from the lack of adequate records and a failure of tradition to "hand over" the full story.

The women of the past cannot tell her what to do now. They can tell her what they faced, what they found themselves capable of. If traditional records can be made to "hand it over," they may reveal to her their personal sense of self. She can then stand where they could not, at the salutary crossroads of truth and love, where feeling for a person and knowledge of the full shape and sweep of that person's life combine, and judgment is purified of both the sentimental and the disengaged. Occasionally, since history is not one endless, steady tide of progress, the women of the past may prick her conscience: some of them have dared more, struggled harder, established capabilities for their sex that have since been forgotten; beachheads have been taken at great price, and then surrendered. Why? Once or twice, perhaps, a rare affinity will remind her that time is not the ultimate "great divide," that ties we do not understand can link us to someone quite removed from us in any predictable way.

It may be, as Mary Daly insists, that the truly great models are "model-breakers," whose effect on others is to inspire them with the courage to affirm their own uniqueness.[4] But it may also be that there is a cumulative wisdom to be derived from the story of women who have preceded us, that they mediate to us the powerful, dynamic category of the feminine as a base for breaking through to new reality.

This book is written out of a sense of women's needs today. But it is also written out of a strong sense of hope. As we learn to ask the right things of and from the past, it will cease to put an oppressive weight on us; it may even offer some support. The role models we choose will not tell us *what* to do. We stand at our point, not theirs, on the overall human trajectory. They can give us more confidence in our power to do what seems best. Only if we abdicate our rightful place by failing to live, decide and act in the present, will the past wield an unhealthy power over us; only if we connive with it in the interests of security, can it cheat us of our future.

The conniving, of course, can take two forms. We can accept the beliefs and practices of the past unquestioningly and try simply to repeat them in our own lives; the comfort of the familiar balances even as it contributes to the staleness and monotony we incur as its price. Rigid forms protect by walling out; they also wall in. The backward glance can paralyze. (cf. Gen. 19:26).

But perhaps we are more likely now to connive by imposing our counter-beliefs and practices upon the past, to lay *our* weight upon it, making it say what we want it to say. Our willfulness betrays a lack of confidence in our own freedom, our ability to create anew. It tells of our fear to trust our experience, our connection with God and with one another. If we were wise, we could relax and allow the past to reveal its own perspectives, without being threatened because they might be different. And having listened (to the *full* past, not simply one sex's view of it), we would be closer to reality—the ground of our hope.

I have tried to listen to the past, not to connive with

it. My own commitment on starting out was to a
dynamic Christian faith which continues to grow in
understanding of its original riches, and which calls its
members to participate actively in unfolding the
fullness of "the Christ that is to be." It was not, as I
have indicated, a commitment of any great depth to
Mary. In the course of writing I have come to realize
how fully I am engaged by this most singular and in
some quarters unpopular of Catholic beliefs. If her
dogmas have not been kept breathing, spontaneous,
life-engendering; if her cult has not evoked intelligent,
adult devotion, it is not she who has failed us. It is we
who have failed ourselves.

In pursuit of a better vision of her in our time, I
found myself drawn into a speculative *circulatio*,
around the woman as she knew herself, as she expressed herself in relationship, and as the Church in
time expressed her—if you will, Mary as Virgin, as
Mother, and as mystical symbol. I do not mean to imply a strict chronological order, for the circle is endless
and ought not to be broken up. Many women have
not succeeded in being one-in-themselves; some have
not yet found the courage to generate life from that
self, still less to shape the symbolic statement they
would want to make to others. In addressing Mary
under these three aspects, the next three chapters
separate them for our sakes. She seems to have
managed a seamless garment.

Chapter One
One-in-Herself

If the circle has a start, it is here. We come into the world the product of many pre-existing forces, our parents, their parents, all the line of begetters before them; our race, our culture, our point in space and time; and in and through all these forces, the shaping hand of One who permitted them and willed us.

And yet without the start that each one of us is individually, there would be no circle—not ours, anyway. It is not a matter of taking credit or boasting without reason; it is not—at first—our decision or our achievement. It is simply a fact: we are individually real, individually called, not from the number of other real human beings, but from the endless throng of possible, imaginary ones. The true "Chosen People" are those who have been given selfhood, given human life. All who are, are chosen. Their individual being by its very diversity tells us something more of the immensity, the scope of their Creator.

The "start" of the circle ought not to be taken lightly.

And yet few reputable books on Mary begin here; not many more include it along the way. This seems a sign of something out of focus in theological and devotional literature concerned with God's Virgin Mother, if not of something incomplete in our relationship with her in itself.

Perhaps it is the latter, and it has been left to our age to contribute here as it has in so many fields, our consciousness of the individual self as an area for concern.

I think more likely it is the former, and Marian literature has failed to record what was in the hearts of many women kneeling before her statue or lighting a candle at her grotto: their conversation with another woman about her life and how she lived it, their private and intuitive concern with her as a person, their wondering about her thoughts, her feelings, her means of coping. If some moved quickly at times to the list of favors they would have her attend to, in view of her heavenly connections, how many more simply left the list with her, their hearts eased by the sharing and the felt presence of a friend. And whether their prayer was one of petition or simple contemplation, if they had read of the theological distinctions among *latria*, *dulia* and in-between degrees of reverence they most certainly would have smiled at the official male Church, so anxious that they not confuse Mary with divinity: only men, perhaps, would give—or need—that warning.

At any rate, theologian after theologian in our day points out the fact that Scripture is not interested in Mary as an individual, but "simply" in her relationship to Christ and the Church.[1] They are at pains to stress the Biblical writers' principle of selection, and to keep their own exegesis from the pitfalls of amateur psychologizing and sentimental piety. They have clearly advanced our understanding of divine revelation and the forms in which it is contained; they first made possible and later elaborated the achievement of Vatican II in connecting Mary in a scripturally-based way to the rest of Catholic belief. In doing all these things, they may also have conveyed the impression that Mary's own self is unknowable to us now, and even if it were known, of minor importance.

We can gather from history that where theology will not "fill in the blank," apocryphal imagination and personal projection will—at the cost, sometimes, of the maturity and dynamism of religious devotion. But then, while professing objectivity and respect for the Scriptural text, more than one theologian has also "filled in the blank," with a Mary so totally functional to man's and God's needs that few modern women can believe in her, let alone imitate her.

Much is, in all honesty, unknowable now. To affirm clearly that we do not know it, and recognize our speculations for the tentative things that they are, is the beginning of wisdom. This same wisdom, however, must lead us to mark out and put a value on what we do not know. For if we regard it as something of minor importance, we will surely never make an effort to recover it and, worse, may feel ourselves free to reach deeply contingent, far-ranging conclusions without it.

Speculation is precarious. Still it seems we need to affirm for our time that Mary had a self, that she was a unique human individual—subject, naturally, to the specifications of her sex, her race, her time in history, to all the forces that precede the "start" of the circle. If

she is, like us, human, then she is, like us, intricately
made, and it is not a sin but a cause for giving thanks,
as the psalmist does; her immaculate conception cannot have flattened her out into a piece of pliable,
unresistant cookie dough, but must have clarified and
endorsed her individual being. We cannot claim to
know this self of hers in great detail—it may be just as
well, as Caryll Houselander says, that we do not, for
some would no doubt miss the meaning and task of
their own individual being by patterning themselves
too literally after her.[2] But for our own integrity even
more than hers, we must put a value on the self that
we do not know, and resist lines of thought that do
not take account of it.

We have always believed that her Son "grew in
wisdom and age and grace"; studies of the developing
Messianic consciousness of Jesus have helped us in
recent years to fit our belief in the Incarnation together
with our knowledge of the human growth process.
The very natural assumption that the mother of Jesus
also developed as a human being has not been so
well explored.

The Task of the Self

Modern psychology has helped us to see what such
development may entail. And yet even today it is not
possible to go very far in the language of selfhood
without coming up against opposite ways of understanding it: Christians have an affinity for linking an
orientation towards the self with an orientation toward

sin, or at least imperfection. The self is the source of "selfishness." Concern with the self is opposed to concern for others. "Self-centeredness" is opposed to "God-centeredness." Even though we believe our humanity has been redeemed, we suspect the self of a deeply-ingrained tendency toward evil, and speak of the spiritual life as a continuous struggle against it. Our means of growth in sanctity is often "self-mortification"; our goal is "self-sacrifice" or "death to self."

But I am using the term "self" in this chapter to include all our individual capacities and potential, conscious and unconscious—the pure and utter gift which is the "start" of the circle, and the full realization of which is the circle's God-destined end. One might think twice about trying to die to this.

We who are Christians sometimes have trouble seeing that having an ego is not the same as being egotistic. In Jungian terms, the "I" or ego is the conscious part of the self: a firmly established ego identity is a necessary step to human adulthood. It is not achieved in isolation; though we speak of the self as an individual entity, we recognize that it grows through relationships, not apart from them. We can also speak of it as a task, for our true self must be sifted out from the variety of false or limited selves suggested to us by the expectations and judgments of others, or by our own mistaken pride. Psychologists call this task the work of individuation. Spiritually, we seem to lack adequate terminology: if we use such phrases as "self-emptying" or "self-sacrifice" to mean abandoning the

task of the self, we have sold our birthright, and for-
saken the one thing no one else can do for us.

In effect, the task of the self is the final stage of
development in the schema of human growth out-
lined by Erich Neumann.[3] Neumann's theory, which
can be applied either to collective or to individual
growth, distinguishes four separate phases of consciousness: 1) the original situation of undifferentiated
consciousness, a kind of participation mystique; 2) the
matriarchate; 3) the patriarchate; and 4) the phase of
individuation. In the first phase, there is no separation
of the self from the Mother or source of being; in the
second, the ego achieves a precarious separation
from the unconscious, but continues to be dominated
by the Mother and seeks only to please her. In stage
three, the ego differentiates itself fully from the unconscious, rejecting the feminine and vesting authority
in the archetype of the Father. In the final phase of individuation, the ego frees itself from the domination
of the masculine as well, and reconciles the psychic
opposites of male and female within itself, establishing
on a conscious level the unity and wholeness that
were potentially present at the beginning. Having
been clearly differentiated, the ego has experienced
the separation necessary for true encounter; it is
finally able not only to connect with the self,
understood as including its "feminine" and unconscious aspects, but to allow this newly-integrated
self to replace it at the center of the personality.

For either sex, the task of the self is a life-long process. It is a moving, not toward narrow individualism,

but toward increasingly fruitful and harmonious connection with the whole of reality. "Between the ego
and the unconscious is born a wider personality,"
writes another psychologist, "and this leads into the
collective, for one's own uniqueness is that particular
way in which collective things have come together."[4]
And like all births, it has a price—the pain of separation, confrontation, loneliness; the sacrifice of
achieved security; the facing down of illusions; the
movement into the unknown.

In the Jungian view of personality, distinctive
archetypes mediate between the ego, the self, and the
collective unconscious: the anima, or feminine archetype, for the man; the animus, or masculine archetype, for the woman. Much has been written on the
anima and her power to evoke the creative, feelingful
life of man's nature, as well as to entangle him in
unreal and dependent fantasies. Less well understood, perhaps, is the role of the animus in the
development of the woman's consciousness, in helping her to focus and shed light on what she already
knows with a diffuse kind of awareness,[5] and enabling
her to concentrate on the long-range goal of individuation, suspending present claims upon her instincts of relatedness and pity.[6] The animus enables a
woman to pull away from an undeveloped, passive
identity with the feminine principle, and establish ego
stability. This is a difficult achievement, for our culture
has not usually encouraged ego development in its
women, while "breaking away from the mother" has
always been considered an important step for the

male. As with the anima, however, the animus has
potential for both good and evil, and can trap a
woman in the phase of the patriarchate, tyrannizing
over her with rational, collective truths which are in-
appropriate for her immediate situation.

Her ultimate goal, the full realization of her self, will
only be reached by coming to terms with the feminine
principle, and striking a conscious balance of the
polarities within her. This is not a passive submission
to a reality which she "should have known all along,"
but a new and dynamic state of being. She wins
through to it by active struggle, in which she consciously chooses to relate herself to the positive
aspects of the "Great Mother," while disobeying the
negative ones. Only Sophia, feminine wisdom, can
help her to discriminate, to make the right sacrifices
and long-range choices.

Neumann's schema is of course a simplification.
Few human lives fall quite so neatly into a pattern.
Yet it does help us to understand some of the confu-
sions experienced by women in our own time, as they
seek to realize their selves in the midst of the breaking
up of a thoroughly patriarchal cultural setting. And it
suggests to us that Mary had a task closely bound up
with bearing the Son of God, yet distinct from it.

The Girl of Nazareth

How far these terms and concepts seem from the
village of Nazareth, even today, and certainly as it
was 2000 years ago. We have evolved them, to be

sure, from stories and legends almost equally ancient. The very notion of an archetype refers to something which manifests itself universally, though in different ways, in every age. But the sophistications of depth psychology, the language of self-realization, concern for inner emotional development, belong to our century—or at least to a humanistic age and culture and not, as Leonard Swidler makes clear, to post-exilic Judaism.[7]

Mary's life, we say, was simpler. A woman's life in any underdeveloped country leaves little time for leisure, little energy for introspection. She performed the timeless, universal tasks by which women kept civilization going for centuries: spinning, weaving, washing, mending, building fires and baking bread. Or, if we place any credence in the apocryphal *Protoevangelium* of James, she may have served in the Temple until she was twelve, the customary time for marriage; in this case, she would have spent her time weaving the Temple curtains.[8]

In either event, there was no doubt about woman's role in her society: Rich or poor, they were handmaids of their men. Their mobility was quite limited; the center of their life was the home, and their main duty was to bear and raise children. Superfluous conversation with them was prohibited, and they were not encouraged to study Torah. In rabbinic writings, they are often grouped with slaves and children.[9]

We can close our eyes and see the Jewish women of her time, dark-haired and dark-eyed, bearing water pitchers to and from the well, one eye peering out

from their required head covering, their thoughts
unknown, because unrecorded.

The "start" of the circle ought not to be taken
lightly.

She was an ordinary woman of her time, at least on
the surface. So ordinary, in fact, that those who knew
her and Joseph could not reconcile this knowledge
with her son's claim to messianic identity.

She had a woman's body, and was subject to its
cycles, its pains, its promises of birth and death. Her
religion had ritualized her very biological rhythms. By
the laws of *niddah,* or ritual uncleanness, she would
have been exiled to a separate existence from her
husband each month during her period, and would be
cleansed each time by immersing herself in the
mikveh, or ritual bath, seven days after the flow of
blood had stopped.[10] The few other time-specified
commandments by which she was bound were also
physical—separating the dough for the Sabbath
loaves, lighting the Sabbath candles.[11] Her whole
spirituality would be centered largely in meeting the
daily needs of her home and family. Over her, on the
eve of the Sabbath, her own father would have pronounced the ancient prayer for a Jewish daughter,
that she would find fruitfulness in the ways of her
fore-mothers: "May God make thee like Sarah, Rebecca, Rachel and Leah."[12] Later in life, her fidelity in
observing the law would lead her, like all Jewish
mothers, to present her son in the Temple, after forty
days of purification.

And like the other people of Galilee, she would

have looked beyond the bounds of her family and the peaceful cycles of her life, at the forces which threatened to disrupt it. We think of Nazareth as a rural village, perhaps with some condescension, remembering Nathaniel's reaction in the Gospel. Yet it was in the midst of a cosmopolitan people, in an area so filled with foreigners that it was called "Galilee of the Gentiles."[13] The district was a center for the movement of Jewish nationalists known as the Zealots, and had already been the scene of an abortive rebellion and retaliation by the Romans.[14] Galilee was no stranger to political or social upheaval, and both men and women of the area were liable to be highly conscious of it. Like everyone else, she would have worried, and been anxious for the news.

Who was Mary of Nazareth?

On one level, beyond these few scattered concrete facts, we cannot go. Modern Biblical scholars have shown us how much even the passages of the Gospel in which she seems most visible are woven out of symbol and legend, and while in their way they tell us truth, their way is not that of historical biography.[15]

In all surface ways, it seems, she was an ordinary woman. But faith and intuition tell us that she was extraordinary too. We work back from the results, the events of her life and that of her son, and say: This is new, this is different, this end was not contained in this beginning—unless there was more in this beginning than we had thought.

The doctrine of the Immaculate Conception as presently formulated has a ring of divine chivalry to it—the raising up of a woman from a "lower class" to make her worthy of God's son, and keep the "immediate family" thoroughly royal and superior. There is an extravagance about the gift, a gratuitousness; it is not surprising that the dogma crystallizes in the West in the High Middle Ages, or that its leading supporters are of the Franciscan school, while some of the most esteemed figures in Christian tradition pronounced against it.[16] To outsiders, when the dogma was proclaimed formally in 1854, it seemed as if the Church itself had been carried away by chivalry, paying its lady a compliment nowhere authorized by Scripture and casting doubt on the universality of the redemption worked by Christ alone. One hundred years after the papal definition tidied things up, many still find the doctrine an encumbrance, and one hardly worth the time spent formulating it.

Especially now. What, after all, does one Marian privilege matter, more or less? The age of chivalry is over, and there is far more practical reason to worry about fixing the time when human life may be said to begin, than when the holiness of one woman did. If she was so generously endowed by God, then she belongs more to him than to us, and we will find our role models elsewhere. Our egalitarian minds have been trained to admire what people make of their lives, rather than the riches they were born with. Besides, innocence is not something we would wish to imitate even if we could; in our minds it is too closely linked to ignorance, and an inhuman kind of detachment, if not to a complete denial of sexuality.

The doctrine has come down to us as an impossible combination of the general and the particular—too particularly something done to *her,* too generally something held out to *us.* We pass.

Perhaps, however, we pass because we have not fully understood the nature of grace and the way it affects the human personality, nor the nature of sin, nor the relationship between the individual and corporate creation. In this case, we pass because the doctrine has been formulated in terms of a previous age, and we cannot see through this veil what it says to us.

Grace is not a measurable quantity, although many of us still struggle to unlearn our deeply-engraved images of stain-free garments, water in pails, years remitted from our personal account in purgatory. Rather, grace is simply the love of God for his creation, which is total and immeasurable. The consciousness of this love wraps us round and draws us on, when we attend and respond to it. We do not "contain" it, but are contained by it. The most powerful of all loves, it is also the most delicate: it does not force, it leaves us free.

The Western idea of original sin has also suffered from an overly physical interpretation. Our understanding was shaped to a large degree by St. Augustine in his struggles against the Pelagian heresy. To Augustine, original sin was an inherited guilt or stain, transmitted inescapably through the sexual act; to the Eastern mind, on the other hand, it was connected more with mortality and general human weakness than with a moral stain or "macula."[17] In modern theology, our approach has been refined by a more personal conception of sin as alienation or estrangement, and therefore of original sin as the corporate alienation of the race from God. In these terms, John Macquarrie suggests, Mary becomes the one who is not alienated, the unquenched spark of "original righteousness"; the privilege of her immaculate conception is better spoken of positively as the presence of grace, than negatively as the absence of sin.[18] To be "immaculate," it should go without saying, does not mean to be spared the effects of a sinful world; as Schillebeeckx puts it, "she too was exposed to all those incalculable and irrational elements common to the human situation—the coming together of inexplicable circumstances, the machinations inherent in communal life, the senseless and harsh conflict of human passions—all of which can lead to the brutal oppression of a totally innocent person."[19] But the oppression could not quench her grace.

Again, "process theology" has helped us to revise our concept of a static and fixed state of holiness. If God's love is infinite, our capacities can never exhaust it; even one called "full of grace" can go on growing and discovering new dimensions in it. Love does not come to an end (1 Cor 13:8) in the next life, still less in this one.

Mary immaculately conceived is not a woman unfree, totally predetermined, sinless because she had no choice. She is not a woman removed, untouched, without knowledge of conflict and suffering. Nor is she inhuman, a fixed, immovable being in the midst of a world of growth and change. If her son was "like us in all things except sin," she can hardly be otherwise.

Far from an idle matter of chivalry, it seems this doctrine touches our deepest sense of what it is to be related to God, and the effect this relation has upon our humanity. Either what was bestowed on her at her conception was a capacity for fuller being, for a richer living out of her gift of life, or we turn God into the wicked fairy, offering a curse under the guise of a birth-gift.

But there is nothing more enabling, more redeeming to the human personality than the knowlege of being loved for what we are. There is nothing which frees us more to be who we are, which liberates us from the fear of revealing ourselves as different, than love. In the end, those who love know, it is "strong as death"—the mortality which the Eastern Fathers identified with original sin—and wipes out every "stain" or imperfection: "you are wholly beautiful, my love, and without a blemish" (Cant. 4:7). And if it can do these things in the end, as Duns Scotus argued, why could it not, just once, do them in the beginning? Thus the Western mind arrived, with its usual torturously slow analysis, at a way of expressing what the Eastern mind intuited more quickly: that there was a unique harmony, an integrity and wholeness in Mary. Her being led God—with his foreknowledge of all that she would choose to do and become—to push the essential collaboration between divine love and human freedom to the very boundary of the finite being's existence, to the core of the finite being's personality.

It was not an act of chivalry by a patriarchal God trying to preserve his pedigree. It was simply the quickness of love knowing its own and calling it forth.

Love walks a dynamic, subtle balance line that the human intellect finds hard to maintain without help. The East responded more quickly to Mary's holiness, but sometimes communicated it as an unnatural exemption from the laws of human nature and development, a powerful and frightening reflection of transcendence invading the human person. Mary's purity makes her a child prodigy in the East. In the *Protoevangelium* of James, she joyfully leaves her parents at the age of three to enter the Temple, where she is fed by angels; Byzantine preachers show an increasing tendency to separate her from normal human life and mold her according to the Byzantine ideal of *apatheia,* or freedom from emotions.[20]

Others, both in the East and the West, follow the opposite direction. They credit her with a human, specifically feminine identity, including what they perceived as common manifestations and failings of the female ego. Irenaeus rebukes her overeagerness at Cana, Tertullian finds her aloof and disbelieving during Christ's public life, Origen believes she was scandalized by the Passion, Chrysostom depicts her as vain and overemotional, even ready to kill herself at the Annunciation. In this view, her holiness is achieved only gradually, through struggle and submission to the guidance of her son.[21]

East and West alike, however they defined Mary's position in the eyes of God, were fairly quick to see her usefulness as a model in the eyes of men—and especially, women. From the 4th century on, both hold her up as the ideal of the consecrated virgin, projecting on to her the norms of the ascetical life of the time, and ignoring historical discrepancies.[22] Belief in Mary's holiness, in effect, mirrors the contemporary human vision of the ideal, or "state of original justice." If emotions or passions are viewed as inherently sinful, then the ideal must be to eliminate them. If division of roles and cultural norms for each sex are conceived as divinely ordained, then an "immaculate one" follows them instinctively and the rest of us do our best to imitate her. The holiness of one has repercussions for all.

We do not today need to be convinced of our own deeply divided natures, nor of the extraordinariness of the human being through whom God became incarnate on our earth: the whole thrust of Christian tradition has been to make these two points very clear. We *do* need to get clear in our minds the nature of the integrity of her person, and the ways that grace and the person interact in time; theologians could help modern women by paying more attention to this, and a little less to the physical integrity of her body. The Church has carefully guarded through the centuries, and in the face of many human efforts to bring it

down to a more human, less numinous level, the
paradox of the Virgin Mother; it has not always been
as careful with the paradox of God's action and ours.

Perhaps it is because she was a woman, and the
notion of the feminine embedded in our minds is that
of the principle which does not act, but receives the
acts of others. Or because we see her, like most
women, immersed in materiality and in time, and
therefore helpless to transcend herself. And/or
because we are so used to thinking of God as male,
the one who takes the initiative. But the transcendent
Being whom Jesus called Father did not always take
initiatives in the way that human men have been ac-
customed to do, imposing himself upon a situation in
total dominance: "My ways are not your ways."
Those who speak of Mary as his mere instrument in-
trude quite roughly upon the nature of their partnership; those who speak of her as his single high point
of creation belie the nature of his unfolding plan, the
patience and the magnitude of it. Both are in a way
right; both are in a more important way wrong.

She had no visions before the Annunciation, nor
after, as far as we know. God took the initiative of
giving her life, and a rich capacity for growing in it.
Once again, twelve years later, he took another initiative. Scripture represents this as the message of the
angel Gabriel; others say it was a mystical experience.
A recent scholar finds it "far more plausible to think
that Mary, who would have been only a young girl
. . . simply felt an overpowering call to place herself
entirely at God's disposal, no matter what it might en-

tail."[23] The hindsight, personal or communal, by which Luke reconstructed the details of her experience, shows us again, at a point when one might expect the divine to be painted as most directive and compelling, how dialogically it operated.

In between, she was left to discover her God in her ordinariness, in her daily life, and her womanhood. Living these realities is not passive; discovering God in them demands that our powers operate at their fullest capacity. If she had not discovered him in them, it seems unlikely that she would have "conceived of conceiving him" in herself, by the Spirit. Trafficking with the infinite is a risky business for one without a solidly established ego identity; becoming "the place where God's transcendence and immanence meet"[24] requires a person with two feet on the ground.

And this brings us back to that unknown, but vital factor, Mary's sense of self. If we assume that the extraordinary grace or love in which she was conceived did not overturn the normal development of her powers and personality, but brought a special clarity and strength to them as they grew, should we not see the Mary who was preparing to marry Joseph the carpenter as a young woman with an increasing unity of body, mind, heart and will, a woman who experienced the goodness of existence, the beauty of nature, the power of love acutely and deeply, one who was in realistic touch with life, and with her self.

To be in touch with one's self—a modern cliche, if there ever was one. And yet we have always held that she was in touch with God. Not necessarily crediting the apocrypha which place her in the Temple since her infancy, we still do insist on her life of contemplation, her knowledge of the Scriptures, the spiritual groundwork of her vocation. We forget, perhaps, that no one can ever really be in touch with God without being in touch with their selves at the same time—and if they are not, there is every reason to believe that what they call "God" is really the self, projected and disguised, a most dangerous delusion.

In assuming that she spent much time in prayer, we forget too that the patterns of her people did not assign this function to the female sex. Jewish women were exempt from the study of Torah and from many time-bound religious duties; responsible as they were for household duties and caring for the needs of their families, they were more properly viewed as the enablers of the prayer life of their men. The image of Mary falters doubly here, for we also envision her as a woman preparing to follow the established patterns of her people—and we hope, the dictates of her heart— in marrying the man approved for her by her father. Was it no more than a marriage of convenience to which she resigned herself? Some speculate that she had made an early vow of virginity, trying to eke out an explanation of what was to come, in terms of what preceded.

Our notions of the spiritual life may lead us to exaggerate the choice we imagine her as having to make. We see prayer as a labor in itself, removed from the concerns of the physical and the everyday, and vulnerable to distraction by them. We assign the serious spiritual life to the scholar and the priest, and lean on them for periodic messages from the divine; for ourselves, our vocation is humbler. We say we know too, of course, that action has its own spirituality, that work is prayer, and that we can "find God in all things"—though we are still trying to figure out how.

On the other hand, hers was a simpler life, we suppose, with more natural rhythms and manual labor that does not tax the mind: her heart would be with God while her hands spun and wove and swept. It is easy to romanticize the primitive, to overlook the back-breaking, heart-sapping labor involved in surviving in an agricultural society. The Jewish law may have been quite realistic in recognizing the limitations on what one human being could accomplish, if narrow and arbitrary in making its distinctions by sex.

And as far as we can see it, there was nothing in the external life of Mary of Nazareth which pointed to a divergence from the traditional role assigned to women in her society—except, perhaps, that she and her husband did not choose to have children beyond her first-born son.

If we hold that internally she was more whole, more unified, more related to herself and to her God than we or the women of her own time, it cannot be on the basis of an idealization of peasant life, or of a projection of fourth century models of consecrated virginity back to first century Judaism. But neither, if she is to have any meaning for us apart from the purely functional role of physical motherhood, can we leave her floating in the realm of special privilege, divorced from the realities and the resources of her human self. It may be that we have to look again at her, and put together what we know in a new way.

A Woman's Way

Divine initiatives, we have said, are not always masculine ones. God is both doer and beholder of his creation, as the author of Genesis knew: he creates, and sees that it is good. He has the capacity to imagine, and so to embody his ideas; afterward, he does not take his creation for granted, but has the capacity to wonder, to marvel, to take delight in it. He speaks, and lets his creation speak back to him. God as artist is one of the earliest images Scripture offers us of the divine. And the artist is the one most closely in touch with the feminine within himself.

Whether the feminine principle is at work in a man or a woman—or a God—it is characterized by a unique combination of the receptive and the active, and a special quality of presence to unconscious processes.

Francoise Mallet-Joris tells us how she writes a novel:

> I am still at the stage of making notes and waiting for something to swim up to the surface . . . I can *feel* what it is that I want to talk about perfectly well . . . I can *feel* what it is, but I do not yet *know* what it is. I must wait.[25]

For the feminine consciousness, in Jungian terms, understanding is not an act of the intellect, quickly sizing up and classifying; it is rather a "conception," in which the ego encircles, considers and ponders the new content, and participates affectively with it before bringing it forth to the world. The knowledge which results is not abstract, nor easily verbalized; it is a kind of comprehension which "grows quietly over a period of time and transforms the person who has it."[26]

When experienced positively, the feminine principle can give the vitality that comes from being caught up in a creative process—ability to be open to new insights, flexibility, playfulness, a sense of facing the future with expectancy and hope.[27] Time for the feminine consciousness is qualitative and cyclic—*kairos*—rather than *chronos,* or a series of equal or similar moments.[28] Matter is indissolubly united with spirit, and the experience of the numinous is historical and individual:

> Religion . . . is not different from ordinary life but is rather an intensification and deepening of it. Perhaps the reason that "woman" and "feminine" have traditionally connoted nature, earth, and sexuality, as if divorced from spirit, is because they have been seen from the viewpoint of the patriarchal head ego which introduces a separating duality between the flesh and the spirit.[29]

Feminine wisdom, the highest expression of the feminine modality of being, is the wisdom of the heart, issuing from one's instincts, one's unconscious, one's history and loving participation in relationships.[30]

We realize, at the same time, that the feminine modality has a double dimension. Waiting can become sheer inertia, or aimless drifting; encircling can become devouring; openness to the unconscious can lead to madness or drunken dissolution. To be at the mercy of one's emotions can lead one to be most unmerciful to self or others. Brutal human sacrifices climaxed the rites of ancient fertility cults.[31] Fear of the feminine idols of the Canaanite religion undoubtedly provoked a counterreaction in the development of the Judaic tradition, and the Roman cult of Cybele, still active in the Christian era, might well have been in the minds of Western Fathers such as Ambrose in the fourth century.[32]

In the ancient myths, the forces of the feminine principle, whether positive or negative, were merged in a single, powerful female figure. The virgin goddess is whole, "one in herself." Her virginity is not physical—her instincts and practices might be, on the contrary, quite promiscuous—but psychological; it refers to an inner attitude. She has a distinct role, and power which does not depend on a husband-god, or indeed on anyone outside her own psyche. She does what she does "not because of any desire to please, not to be liked, or to be approved, even by herself; not because of any desire to gain power over another, to catch his interest or love, but because what she does is true."[33] Awesome in her autonomy, she represents the impersonal, unpossessable feminine principle, beyond conventionality and beyond egoism. Women who worshipped her recognized and took the responsibility for their own instinctual life upon themselves, through ritual acts which expressed the power of these instincts while renouncing all claim to possessiveness over them.[34]

But we are a long way from the agricultural societies over which a fertility goddess could exercise such mysterious and total power. Virginity, whether physical or psychological, is no longer seen as wholeness, but as incompletion. Married or unmarried, modern woman has read her society's message that intellect makes the world go round; one can make rain with chemicals, conquer the moon with computers, and control female generativity with a pill. She does not trust her emotions any more than modern man trusts his—perhaps she trusts them less, for they seem to have betrayed her into his control, and a position of inferiority.

Again, the solution can not be a matter of romanticizing the primitive, but of pushing through to a new state of being in which we learn to connect the feminine principle and all its powers appropriately with the complementary principle and powers of the masculine. Obviously, this means new ways of relating and cooperating between men and women. But it also means looking at how the masculine and feminine principles intersect within each one of us. Woman's

problem today, as Anais Nin saw it, is not to make
herself heard so much as it is to hear herself—to
understand what it is that needs expression.[35] Perhaps
it is man's problem too. Sophia does not walk around
in the flesh very often. Neither does Zeus.

Annunciation and Reply

A Jewish girl of twelve or thirteen prepares herself
to be given in marriage. This will be for her, as for
most women, a *kairos*—a moment of time which is
special, when change and otherness confront her,
sharpening her sense of all that she is and has
become, and her energies and feelings gather to a
center within her. Her memories of life as it had been
for her, and her perceptions of the world around her
now are clear, even luminous. Human history and
her own story criss-cross; the great and the small
come together. The great does not make the small
seem trivial, the small does not make the great seem
distant and uncontrollable.

She sits in the part of the synagogue reserved for
women on the Sabbath, and listens to the story of her
people, the Promise, the journeying, the infidelities,
the forgivings. She hears of their heroes, Abraham,
Isaac Jacob, and takes in more intently now, perhaps he stories of Sarah, Rebecca, Rachel, Hannah,
the mothers of the race. Removed from us, they are
close to her—like them, she draws water from the ancient wells, weaves cloth, tends the fire, feels the

blessing of the Lord Jahweh upon the human love which increases and multiplies itself in child-bearing. But unlike her, some of them were old, or barren, and had to badger God into allowing them to conceive. She is young, and Joseph loves her. God too.

If the world only knew how much God loved it, as she does. If it only knew how good it is, how simple, to love back, as she is finding. Kings and judges come and go, nations rise and fall; the main line of life is not always official, public, matter for history books. It is here, in the core of the human spirit, the human heart, among people, and between them and God. But the world does not know this. God will have to press his case more effectively. He will have to send his love into the world.

Others knew this too. But they were older, and their wisdom, like their longing, came from much more life experience than hers—people like Simeon, Anna, her cousin Elizabeth. Her instincts were fresh, more vulnerable, braver: she had a life to fling away by trusting them.

In the *kairos* that has come down to us as the Annunciation, Mary experienced as no one had before in history the immense and surging tide of her Creator's love. And she experienced it as a question—a question from the transcendent, directed at her. This much we know.

Volumes have been written, discussing each word of the angel's message and her reply. The form in which Luke casts it is a literary device, carefully constructed to evoke memories of the Old Testament, and balance the earlier annunciation to Zachary. The experience has been pared to its essentials and stylized. Who is to say an angel really came, spoke his brief message to her, and left immediately with her reply? Who is to say she was alone at prayer in her room at the time, as so many artists have depicted her? (The *Protoevangelium* of James, in fact, has a two-part scene, in which she hears the angel's voice at the well, and then withdraws to her room, where the message is completed.) Who is to say what force, whether inside or outside of herself, a line from Scripture, a rabbi's word, or Joseph's, or some happening in her village triggered what she knew of God and of herself and brought that which she knew into the light?

Whenever and however it was, her moment of realization carried her out of herself, opened her in a stunning way to the needs and hopes of human kind and to the power of God to answer those needs and hopes. Some make her fiat sound so self-abdicating, almost painful, an act of tremendous mortification and resignation, akin to that of her son years later in the garden of Gethsemane. But the Latin veils a difference that is apparent in the Greek; more than a declaration of humble submission, her words are an earnest wish, and a cry of joy.[36]

Before she utters it, she questions and discerns. There is more here than an image from the collective unconscious, or a woman's intuition of a redeeming connection with the transcendent—these may have eased the way, but no matter how many pagan gods visited mortal women in the ancient myths, this is new, this is real, this is no myth. There is more here even than the fulfillment of the promise of the Messiah to her own people. Does she sense this? The words of the angel as Luke records them are ambiguous; "son of the Most High" is more than ordinary Messianic language. There is personal risk here for herself and for her future with Joseph: the penalty in Jewish law for a woman who committed adultery was death by stoning, and though by the first century this was likely to be mitigated, it was still not regarded lightly. If she looks for role models, there is more here than fits the pattern of any earlier woman of her race. This is not a natural, simple, long wished-for conception like Sarah's or Hannah's, nor an act of national military or political bravery like Judith's or Esther's; it is Sarah and Hannah and Judith and Esther mixed together, and then some.

There is more here, no doubt, than one person—or all the race—can comprehend at once. But she comprehends enough to make a decision, and to place herself in a position of active responsibility for this new venture, a position of collaboration with the power of the Most High. Human history and her own story criss-cross; the great and the small come together. The great does not make the small seem trivial, the small does not make the great seem distant or uncontrollable.

And the Word of the Most High was flesh.

With whom could she share this miracle? With Joseph, surely, who was most deeply affected by it; all the laws of justice in human relationship and human love must lead us to believe this.[37] What she could not tell him was his own responsibility in the matter. Like her, at first he feared, and in his dream came to see the even more extraordinary part of this strange event—that it was to be inserted quietly into the ordinary context of their lives together; she was to be no Vestal Virgin, living publicly in a sacred place while all the world adored her son; their mutual love was to be the shelter of the boy marked out for greatness.

And with Elizabeth, wife of the priest Zachary and her kinswoman, to whom she goes in haste. Tradition sees this visit as a sign of Mary's generosity and concern for a pregnant older relative, but it must have helped her too, by removing her from the curiosity of a small village, and giving Joseph time, perhaps, to know his own mind and the divine will for him. The angel had called her attention to Elizabeth as a source of strength and confirmation for her. It could well be, as Professor Ford suggests, that Elizabeth was the first to understand Mary, and so to help her understand herself; it may be too, that the parents of John the Baptist enabled her to connect her personal calling with the religious and political conditions of Israel, for both the Benedictus and the Magnificat have the ring of Zealot hymns.[38]

Outside of this small circle, she did not make the miracle known. We may speculate as to when and how she shared the truth with her son; clearly it was before the scene of confrontation between them in the Temple. But otherwise the secret of Christ's birth was kept so well that his own relatives did not know it; no special reverence marked their attitude toward him when he began his public ministry—indeed, they seem to have been positive impediments (Mk. 3:20-21), basically hostile to his vision and purposes.

A virgin birth is one thing; a life of virginity is something else. If we can pierce through the centuries of Christian writing and preaching on Mary as model for the virgin state, we will see that history has condensed two separate elements of her story. For nowhere in Luke's account does the angel directly counsel Mary as to her future relationship with Joseph; the choice of perpetual virginity is not described *per se* in the Gospel. Indeed, we have reached a point of sophistication in our own culture where Christ's divinity is not seen as hinging on whether or not he had "real" brothers and sisters, or just an extended family of relations. Tradition nevertheless has held from the third century that a life of celibate love was Mary's response to the divine gift made her in the Incarnation.

Without challenging this appropriateness, we can try to focus for ourselves more clearly the dynamic of virginity as choice and witness. The mystery will withstand analysis, if there is any depth to it.

It would be most especially here that Mary had no role models, and little support from her own tradition. Sarah, Rebecca, Rachel, Hannah, Ruth—all sought to serve the Lord by joining themselves to men. Even the women who emerged as heroes in their own right, whether in history or in legend—Deborah, Esther, Judith—did so after marrying. There is evidence that the Essene community at Qumran did believe in and practice celibacy as a part of their way of life, but their sect was small; there is no evidence that Mary knew of them directly.[39] If her virginity had any sign-value to most Jews, it would only have been as a "sign of contradiction."

Nor would this have been a choice involving only herself. Technically, at least, according to Jewish law, it was a decision to be made by her husband.[40] Bit by bit, perhaps, the meaning of what they knew bore in upon them—that singled out for something new, they were to explore the boundaries of a new kind of being in return. We speak of celibacy for the Kingdom; for them the concept of the Kingdom must have been unclear, mixed as it was by so many with political and national overtones, not the universal, cosmic convergence we have come to envision. Celibacy for a future reason of any kind was probably not their thought, nor celibacy for any strictly logical effect, such as greater efficiency, or simply as a sacrifice for more striking testimony to the marvel of the Messiah. Still less, celibacy for fear of sex, or because they could not allow themselves to love. Their lives would not be lived in isolation from each other, but in close proximity and collaboration.

Their choice was as new as their gift. It was celibacy for here, for now, for this overwhelming love that looked them in the face. No sense of heroics about it, perhaps, and yet an act, a choice, that defined their selves as boldly, as radically as that of any hero. An act that was, if you will, more for themselves than for their son, to shape their existence along the lines of the central intuition that had come to them, to embody it. And in being for their selves, it was simply and naturally for their son as well: few others even knew of it, really, during his lifetime, but it was a part of his consciousness and his call. There were two close to him who knew of his origin, and could affirm it to him no matter what happened, two who had made a space for him, and so freed him to search for an "original" way of embodying *his* destiny.

In doing this, perhaps quite unconsciously, they marked out a new boundary of the possible for humanity—a physical and psychic virginity which moves all other forms of human love relationship more clearly into the zone of human choice, rather than compulsion. Their fresh and unconventional response to the experience of God's dealings with them signals their ability to act out of the deepest center of their personalities with both spontaneity and purpose, moving away from tradition and previous role models which did not fit their truth.

We say this was a joint decision. But we can't help

noticing, too, that it bears the earmarks of the anima, or in Mary's case, the feminine self: it is a unique response to a unique personal situation, a refusal to be bound by the either-or categories in which the animus frequently frames conflicts,[41] or by collective and conventional opinion. As a solution it is not artificially or intellectually created, but organic. In reconciling opposing loyalties to a moral code and to love, it has been said,

> in the last analysis no theory will serve for a woman of deep integrity. . . . Certain women who have attempted in this simple and sincere fashion to live their lives to the best of their ability, see on looking back over the period of perplexity and blindness how each step which they took fitted into a whole, invisible at the time, but making at the end a complete and amazingly apt solution of what seemed at the time to be an impasse. Had it been consciously worked out, the end result might have been called clever. Inasmuch as it evolved of itself out of a facing of the difficulties, it can only be called clever in the same sense as can a vine which finds its way through a stone wall into the light.[42]

We speak perhaps too much of the "mystery" of the choice of celibacy—and this is a sign of our sense of total inadequacy to explain it on a rational level. What we ought to be speaking about is its complexity—insofar as when authentic it originates from the deepest center of the human psyche and integrates the multitudinous elements of body and soul in a way that makes a computer's workings seem simple by comparison—and the mystery of each human individual, expressed in their life choices of whatever kind. Mary was not "one-in-herself" *because* of her choice to be virgin, but because God had made her whole and unique in creating her, and grace and nature had combined to enable her to develop this potential. Her choice—and Joseph's—to express their wholeness in celibacy reflects their faith in the value of their personhood before God, and a primary love relationship which like a vine "finds its way through a stone wall into the light" in its own way.

A choice of direction in life is just that—the beginning of a journey. One's capacities for unity, self-knowledge, responsible exercise of one's gifts, may be given a new depth and impetus by a life decision, but the story is far from over. Time confers new understanding on what was initially done, though only in response to an inner work of sifting and weighing—the work of "pondering" to which Mary was given. It is one of the few things we are told directly about her in the Gospel, and we can gain a better understanding of obedience, and of her relationship with God, by noting the care that Luke takes to make this point. The Eastern Fathers played with the notion of her unified response to the Annunciation as the "hearing womb"—the attentive, actively receptive, nourishing environment of the Logos, which builds up and brings into bodily being the divine reality.[43] The paradox of "a womb which hears" reminds us of the role played by her mind and heart, as well as her body, in this birth. Listening closely to the voice of God speaking through the happenings of her life, she responded as completely as she could from her own self, not automatically, but with contemplative and loving deliberateness—the kind of response that Jesus was to learn from her, and that was to shape his own prayer life. No doubt, though on a different level, the mutuality which marked his dialogues with his Father also marked hers—though patristic literature, bound by incomplete notions of the feminine as naturally silent and passive, failed to develop this.

The Correct Death

Time calls us not only to understand the past but to move into the future, re-establishing the self again and again in relation to changing reality. The Jungian paradigm of growth toward wholeness includes the notion of the need for sacrifice: Psyche must forego her premature paradise and experience all the pain of individuation, the consciousness of self as something other than the partner who is the object of her love; she must face loneliness and death to win life and a complete, fully conscious, mutual love.[44] The ego must die in order for the self to become an actual experience.

Not every death is the "correct death," however; unless a woman's tasks and sacrifices are designed by the feminine principle, as in the Psyche myth, she risks the possibility of surrendering in the wrong place.[45] Most especially when her animus has helped her to move away from an unquestioning identification with the feminine, she is liable to fall victim to that animus, and turn her life over to the service of an idea or cause. Sacrificing for such an object may be noble, but it is incomplete; the potentialities of the self have been diverted into an area which cannot "give them back from the grave," reformed and renewed. Fanaticism, whether in man or in woman, seldom leads to creative solutions. Still less does masochism, the unselective self-sacrifice of a woman who has not stood apart from and critically inspected the feminine principle to begin with; that is, a woman who neither knows nor is free to assert herself, and who seems by her total openness and acceptance of the will of others to invite *them* to be selfish at her expense.

Even in this Jungian frame of reference, it is easier to say what "correct deaths" are *not*, than what they are. No death comes coupled with an instantly visible creative solution; if it did, we would not experience it as a death to begin with. But seeing the experience through can lead us to say that sacrifices which are related to the realization of principles at the very core of our being will in time define themselves as fruitful, even if not in the way that we predict or hope. The wisdom and self-knowledge hidden in the unconscious wells up, whether through dreams, intuition or a process of analysis. Those who have successfully fought the temptation to succumb to either the matriarchal or patriarchal principles as absolute and arbitrary definers of their being will have built up the courage and power to hand their ego identity over to the correct death, beyond which waits their full self.

One can accept the Jungian concern that a woman's tasks and sacrifices be assigned by the feminine principle, without wishing to confine these assignments to women alone. Insofar as Sophia is concerned with the unity and integration of both sexes, she also calls men to move out of fixed, underdeveloped and one-sided stages of being. It goes almost without saying that those of either sex who undertake to act on behalf of feminine values in modern society will call down enough resistance, hardship and mockery upon themselves to constitute a formidable sacrifice—as should be evident from the one who bound these values into his own message in Jerusalem and Galilee, at the beginning of the Christian era.

Journeying to Jerusalem

In the Christian experience too, time tests and probes the self: pain is part of life, sacrifice part of love. The potential for wholeness is given; the achievement of it comes through conscious struggle. We sail forth in hope and self-affirmation, and limp back into harbor broken and very much in need of mending.

Life treated Mary no more gently than us, and she did not have a papal proclamation hanging on her kitchen wall to assure her that she was sinless and free from error. She travelled on in the dark of faith, and there had to be nights when prayer was all a cry from her and no answer from beyond—times such as her son himself knew on the cross.

The Gospels suggest some of her dark moments to us. Obviously, those that touched her son touched her too, and the last months of his public life were marked for both of them by the shadows of the approaching storm. But there were others which seem to have been even more hers than his. After the glow and jubilation of the tales of the wonders of the birth, in fact, Scripture records mostly moments of disturbing challenge for her—Simeon's prophecy of the sword which will pierce her soul, the three days' loss of the child in the Temple, the apparent rebuke at Cana, the rather blunt and unfeeling remarks of Jesus about her to the crowds. Many attempts have been made to explain these last away as actually tender compliments to her faith; none is completely convincing.

Early hopes make us vulnerable. Having moved away from a complete and natural identification with a traditional feminine role, was she tempted to get caught up in her son's cause as Messiah? "My hour is not yet come"—Jesus' comment to her at Cana is formulated, as were many of his sayings preceding the performance of a miracle, as a teaching to draw attention to the true spiritual significance of his mission.[46] His comments about her to the crowds fall under the same category: "still happier are those who hear the word of God and keep it" (Lk. 11:28); "anyone who does the will of God, that person is my brother and sister and mother" (Mk. 3:35). It may be, as John McKenzie suggests, that these sayings are part of the primitive teaching of the Church going out of its way to stress spiritual rather than blood relationships with Christ, and so to prevent his kinsmen from an undue degree of influence in the early Christian community.[47] Whether Mary needed these clarifications herself is highly doubtful. If she ever confused her son's messianic nature with a political cause, her mode of participating in it was strangely indirect. Other women are far more active within Christ's company of disciples; even at Cana, her presence seems to have been at least initially separate from theirs. In the schema of John's Gospel, her life merges with his briefly at the time of his first miracle and again at the end. In between we do not know the role she chose to play; nor again do we know the particular stages of the development of her own faith.

All we can affirm is that it did develop. She did not understand everything immediately, we are told—but surely the long years of what we call the "hidden life" brought insight. Jesus' ideas and teachings as publicly expressed hardly erupted full-blown, without private preparation and exchange.

She could not have been blind to the challenge he was raising to the established structures of her faith, nor to the power of those structures to retaliate. The fate of John the Baptist alone would frighten as well as grieve her; in her tears would be mixed memories of the day of his birth and terror at the ease with which a whim could end a life so intertwined with that of her own son. The tension between her son and other members of the family must have been a further source of suffering; and if this tension carried over into the post-Resurrection church which was his living body, the dissension and rivalry must have angered her even as the jealousy and profiteering in the Temple angered Christ.

No group or institution kept pace with the newness in her life. Always, she is thrown back on her own resources, and her own self's knowledge of the love of God. And what makes us more vulnerable, self-given, indifferent to risk, than love? We do not really find "the correct death." If we are true to our instincts, it finds us. Standing by a cross while her son and God is killed before her eyes, his body and his soul ripped apart and most of his followers nowhere in sight, is death enough for one woman.

There is no pain in the Old Testament, no dying of the self or grief, which surpasses that of Rachel mourning for her children and refusing comfort. There are scars on the heart, as on the body, that seem as if they must endure even in the risen life.

Who was Mary of Nazareth?

She was a real person, a woman of her time, with a woman's heart, and way of feeling deeply; with a woman's mind and way of knowing; with inner resources of memory, imagination, and dream, with courage to hear the new and act on it, to make decisions about her life and relationships, to change her mind when it seemed right, to collaborate closely with a partner, and to stand loneliness when she had to, to keep on going when all seemed lost within her heart and without. If someday, in a way unforeseen by us now, it could be proved to the Christian community that she did not choose perpetual virginity for her way of life, it could not change the impression of integrity, purpose and faith which lead us to call this woman "one-in-herself."

Chapter Two
Bearing Life

From life comes life—physical, psychological, spiritual. Our selves are unique, distinct; they are not alone. As they are created by the selves who touch them along the way, so they reach out and help to shape others too. Sometimes we are especially conscious of a flow of energy in one direction—to us from a parent, a teacher, a person with more faith or wisdom; from us to our children, a student, a person in distress. Sometimes the energy flows both ways, in a deep friendship, a community of equals, love. We need the courage to be as a whole, an individual; we also need the courage to be as a part of a larger whole, without fear of compromising what makes us unique and different. We need to deal with otherness, without losing ourselves in it, or absorbing it into ourselves. We need to learn how to express ourselves in relationship, in a way that will engender life.

We need these things personally; one of the gifts—and perils—of life in the 20th century is that we know we also need them corporately, and even on a cosmic scale. The most hardened non-believer among us has seen what Christ's own apostles did not see, still less John the Baptist or the great patriarchs of the Old Testament—the raw material of the cosmic Christ: the little blue planet earth, gleaming in the darkness from a spaceship window; the black and brown and yellow and white faces of the human race, alive and close-up by TV satellite, with instant translation making sense of the babel of languages; London, Paris, Vienna, Rome, Hanoi and Moscow, Cairo, Johannesburg, and Tel Aviv. The more we look, the more we fear the cosmic Calvary to which we have the power to bring it.

For all our talking about it, we are not very good at relationships on any level and much better at the technology which can capture and measure our failures. We may even exaggerate our guilt over that of earlier ages, for we see so quickly and graphically the dying young soldier, the starving child, the helpless poor staring blankly out of the TV screen into our affluent living rooms. We would like to change the world if we could, but we do not know how; we are not smug, we are impotent. Our feelings and our intelligence do not connect; for our sanity we separate the personal and political spheres, and try to render justice and love to those with whom we live and work, and money if we can spare it to the conduits for the less fortunate, who do not travel the same roads as we to Jericho.

The personal sphere is not always that simple either. Our commitments run out of steam, or those of our partners; our children rebel and accuse us of not caring, or of caring too much; our elders turn bitter and prophesy woe. A woman thinks about bearing a child, and then she thinks again. Never in history, perhaps, have church and society harped so much on the child as "her" responsibility, and never has she been so isolated from help and support as she is now in the modern, nuclear family—unless it is when that nuclear family breaks up and she is left divorced, abandoned or widowed with "her" responsibility.

We need courage to be able to generate life. We need wisdom to know how to do it. We need to couple concern with detachment, rather than possessiveness, toward our children, and toward all the human beings whose lives we touch, to whom we give energy. Male and female, we need to learn to "mother," that is, call forth and nourish their unique free selves—and if the idea of "mothering" is too hopelessly linked up with domination and dependency, then we must scrap it and find a new one for our capacity to relate with creative tenderness to the others in our world. But perhaps we ought not to scrap it before we have given it a fair chance to survive, before we have put the Motherhood of God up alongside the Fatherhood, as inseparably and divinely sanctioning the unity of justice and love, the kiss of kindness and truth that is the sign of the kingdom both personal and political.

Giving Birth

A woman waits for the birth of her child. She is not idle—she is working harder, if anything, to help her older kinswoman, who is further along in her pregnancy—but she moves more slowly. There is inner work to be done as well as outer. Her hands sift the flour and knead the yeast into the dough, patiently, thoroughly, as a man might later work the yeast of a small new community into the wider world. She spins and weaves new cloth, her eyes concentrated on the threads, the pattern; patching old garments, she gauges relative strength and tension, as a man might later gauge the capacity of his audience to receive unexpected good news. Meanwhile her body sifts and kneads and weaves the child. So does her mind.

Marie-Louise von Franz has pointed out how much the process of giving birth on any level is connected with the idea of spinning and weaving, bringing natural elements together in a certain infinitely complex order; producing a child is a "mystery of feminine weaving," both physical and psychological:

> It seems to me . . . that it is essential and positively important for the child that the fantasy of a pregnant woman and mother should in the early stages be centered round the child. I would say that if a mother thinks a lot about the child to come, prays and has fantasies about it, i.e., spins and weaves for it, this fantasy activity prepares a nourishing ground for the child to be born into. . . . Invisible foundations have much to do with the creation of a life situation.[1]

The early Fathers stressed the psychic and spiritual aspects of Mary's motherhood to the point of projecting perhaps a little contempt at its physical reality. Her loving motherhood "would have profited little," wrote Augustine, "had she not first conceived Christ in her heart, and only then in her womb."[2] She "conceived God in her mind before she conceived him in her body," Pope St. Leo pointed out.[3] Mind and heart affirmed, supported and made possible the Incarnation. In different ways we too hail the freeing of motherhood from the realm of biological necessity into the realm of will and choice, although our sense of the interplay between body and spirit is also more complex.

Insofar as it depended upon her prior spiritual realization and consent, her physical act of bearing her child was voluntary and freely-willed. Perhaps, Sidney Callahan speculates, such a unified and self-aware state of mind did actually result in the "miracle" of painless childbirth—no miracle, but the relaxed and joyous confidence of one who felt herself loved and full of grace.[4] Church tradition held the pains of childbirth to be part of the curse incurred by original sin (Gen. 3:16); but long before the doctrine of the immaculate conception itself was clarified, Mary was held to be exempt from the common lot of pain by reason of her miraculous virginity in the very act of childbirth itself. Tradition has never held that her life was otherwise free of pain or suffering, however, and has not spoken decisively about whether she experienced death. It seems that we might also be open to the possibility that once miraculously conceived, Jesus came into the world through the normal processes of a woman's labor—a struggle filled with pain, as he himself was later to remind the apostles, but a pain forgotten in the resulting joy (John 16:21-22).

In making his reference, Jesus had available to him two distinct uses of the pains-of-childbirth metaphor which was applied to Israel in the Old Testament, one stressing the acute distress of the suffering as a sign of God's anger and punishment for sin (Isaiah 13:8; Jer. 13-21; 22:23); the other bringing out the relation of the sufferings to salvation and imminent deliverance (Mich. 9:9-10; Isaiah 66:7).[5] He chose the latter.

God and Mary had been collaborators from the moment of the fiat. Her active collaboration in the birth-scene at Bethlehem should not detract but add to the glory of the Incarnation. But her own son had integrated the positive reality of the birth process into his picture of life in a way which Church tradition proved unable to match; concerned above all with protecting faith in Mary's physical virginity, and so in her son's divine origin, it sacrificed for centuries any possibility of meaningful human cooperation in the circumstance of his birth.

Again, we can only imagine the psychic birthing that she and Joseph gave their son, the care they took to oversee his human growth, helping him to discover the world around him and his own capacities, teaching him by their faithful, nurturing presence to trust in them and in himself. Their home was a sphere of newness, both that which always comes from the fresh vision of a child and that which came from their sense of the divine capacity to surprise and innovate. Having been thus surprised, their vision too was fresh and childlike, and mirrored back to him a basic love of life and hope for each new day to come.

Clearly they brought him up within the Jewish tradition, and shared with him the history of their people and the Promise. At some point too, when he seemed ready, they shared with him his own history, as they knew it, and gave him an even more profound foothold on his identity.

To a son, simply in being what she is, his mother transmits a uniquely potent image by which he receives and interprets the reality of all women. We cannot help but ask where Jesus found the freedom, the ease, the natural friendliness and dignity with which he treated the other women of the Gospels; we cannot but conclude that Mary passed on to him the experience of her own wholeness and humanity in a way which liberated him from the narrow social presumptions governing relations between the sexes. Whatever her personality—whether she was mostly silent, or quite uninhibited in expressing herself, was serious or gay, calm or lively, whether she was the woman he remembered sweeping the house from top to bottom to find a single coin, or one who spent more time contemplating sunsets and lilies in the field, or one who did both—she endowed him with enough basic trust and openness to relate well with women of almost every temperament and background. Theologians may argue about her power, and how to formulate the nature of her intercession correctly; but there can be no argument about this power and the intercession which takes place in the dim, pre-rational levels of the human psyche.

Mothering a Messianic liberator meant not keeping him from the world, but putting him in the closest touch with the political, economic and social realities of his country, as well as its religious history. How often did they talk about the future, weaving the picture of a time when poverty and injustice would be overcome, and the people would be free at last? How many of the parables of the Kingdom did he try out on her—or she on him—before the disciples ever heard them? How much knowledge of life, of everyday experience, of women and of men, did he absorb before feeling ready to put himself to the test and begin his public life of mediation between the world and God? We call these years "hidden," forgetting that a whole adult career is contained in them, and the development of all the inner resources that saw him through his public life and flowed out so richly on to those he met.

Letting Go, and Going On

At some point too, within the span of their days at Nazareth, is contained a turning point, a time when she had to face the fact that a new relationship had evolved, that her son was ready to stand on his own and take full responsibility for his life. Having poured her energy into this channel, perhaps to the exclusion of all others, she had to learn to redirect it. Perhaps the realization came as a jolt; perhaps it grew slowly over a period of time.

The episode of the three days' loss in the Temple would have served warning. By the beginning of the public life she certainly has grasped it, for she does not seem to follow him "on the road"; she allows other women to take over the work of ministering to his needs. Her presence at Cana is obviously an act of friendship to the bride and groom, as is evidenced by her sensitivity to their plight; the context of the original Cana story may well have been popular speculation about the "hidden life," and possible miracles of Jesus *en famille.*[6] If her request pushes Jesus into a new stage of his ministry, it is not that she has made calculated plans to achieve this; she is simply shown as calling his attention to something which a woman of the Jewish culture would have been more likely than anyone else to notice. The Evangelist has discerned a profound symbolic meaning in the incident on a theological level, and presented it in such a way as to bring this out; attempts to read it too closely on a psychological level are risky. The fact remains that although Mary leaves the wedding with Jesus and the disciples, her physical presence is not mentioned again in John's Gospel until Calvary. A new stage of growth entails a break, and cannot be achieved without it.

Whether the "rejection" texts are authentic sayings of Jesus or later additions, the depth of his mother's

dispossession is made clear by Christ over and over
again in the Gospels: To those who left home, brothers or sisters, mother, father or children, he promised
a hundredfold (Mk. 10:29-30); he spoke of bringing
not peace but a sword, and setting family members
against each other (Matt. 10:35-36); no man would
be worthy of him, he warned, who cared more for
father or mother than for him (Matt. 10:37). His call
did not leave time to say goodbye to people at home;
one should not look back, with one's hand on the
plough (Lk. 9:61-62).

We call it dispossession, for this is what it would be
for a woman of a strongly maternal type, one whose
whole identity has been caught up in her child. And
this, we assume, is exactly what Mary was—for could
God have wanted any other kind for His only son?
The maternal woman makes space in her body, her
heart, and the environment around her for her child
to grow in; she shelters, protects and strengthens her
offspring with her spontaneous and unreserved love;
the depth of her commitment is the best human yard-
stick which divinity can use to express its own infinite
care for its creatures: "Does a woman forget her baby
at the breast, or fail to cherish the son of her womb?
Yet even if these forget, I will never forget you"
(Isaiah 49:15). On the other hand, such a woman
sometimes finds it hard to think of herself apart from
her relationship to her children, and impossible to say
"no" to them without guilt. She identifies herself with
her maternal instinct so totally that she cannot tolerate
conflict or apparent failure in the maternal role. Her

superabundant, generous, whole-hearted "yes"—the emblem and meaning of mother love throughout time—may be in reality a compulsive and unbalanced response.

If there is one word with which Mary is identified throughout time, it is her "yes" at the Annunciation. We speak too glibly, perhaps, of this fiat, forgetting the "if's" and "but's" that preceded it. We should remember the power to say "no" implicit in her basic freedom—and also the fact that sons of mothers who always say "yes" do not usually emerge with the courage, decisiveness and controlled aggressiveness of Jesus, the founder of the Christian religion.

In fact, looking at her son, we can well imagine Mary as a woman with her own ability to assert herself, even to differ with him, and to be so strong in her own life and relationship with the Father that her son was empowered to assert *his* independence and follow *his* call without guilt or hesitancy. If she ever did "argue" with him, at Cana or elsewhere, it was not a power struggle, but a matter of being faithful to her vision and her values; if she did come seeking him with relatives who thought he had gone berserk, this is not to say she agreed with their judgment—she might very well have wanted to see for herself, to be able to deal effectively with their criticism. She would not be the only mother in history to have pressure put on her to reason with a revolutionary son—and she would indeed be lucky if the only pressure came from relatives.

But she would be the only mother in history to

have known so clearly from the moment of conception that her son did not belong to her, that his origin
and destiny were mysteriously beyond her, that he
was "owned" by God though entrusted to her for a
time. And the only mother in history to know so
clearly that she too was "owned" only by God, and
not by human love, whether spousal or maternal,
though both of these were richly given her. The one
who gave birth also learned to let go; in doing this,
she tells us all, whatever our style in life, that love can
be freedom, not enslavement, for ourselves and those
we love. If she was "dispossessed" of a role, it was
not the whole of her identity; the implication of the
"rejection" texts is that under all the roles she played
was the primary identity of the woman of faith, hearing God and responding, as she had before her son
was ever conceived.

And going on. If she was not ministering directly
alongside of her son in his public life, we ask, what
was she doing? Here again we face a blank. We may
choose to fill it with pious images of long hours in
prayer, or humble service in the ordinary tasks of life.
Either is possible; it does seem as if her son's message
would have kindled her to an even deeper concern
for people, as she had kindled something by pointing
out their needs to him. She did not have to be with
Christ in order to live like him a life of active Christian
ministry, concerned for widows, orphans and the
ever-present poor. Even before the Sermon on the
Mount, she had probably foreshadowed to Christ the

Christian "way"—making peace, tendering mercy, calling fervently for justice.

There was no one arbitrary role assignment to the women of the Church in the New Testament times, until the anti-feminism of their environment filtered into the institutionalizing process late in the first century.[7] As we see from Acts and the earlier Pauline epistles, women are deacons (Rom. 16:1) and prophets (Acts 21:9; Cor. 11:5), as well as wives, mothers and housekeepers.[8] Whatever role Mary worked out for herself during her son's lifetime or after the Resurrection does not make the other roles less valuable, or less possible. Nor need we assume that she filled only one role. "Going on" in a lifegiving way suggests something more open to change and development: just as her conception of her own religion was altered by her growing understanding of Christ as God and man, so her response may well have flowered on many levels into a rich and creative life in the Christian community, and not that of a queen mother or royal figurehead.

Helping with the Self

One of the images which Church tradition has most often attached to Mary is that of the "new Eve," who aided Christ as the new Adam in the work of redeeming the race from the sin of our first parents. It is not an image which speaks very powerfully to the modern woman, who has trouble accepting the image of the "old Eve" for anything other than an expression of man's fear, hostility and penchant for projecting his own moral failures onto a woman to begin with. And in fact, the analogy does break down in this projection: the ultimate blame is placed on Eve, but Mary can only be allowed a supporting role in the redemptive act.

Misunderstanding of the two accounts of the Creation in the Book of Genesis is not only a sign of the alienation between the sexes, but an efficient cause of its perpetuation. In the older, Yahwist account (Gen. 2:18-25), woman is created last, as the decisive expression of human superiority over the purely animal level, and together she and man form a perfectly related human society, differentiated from each other but not estranged. In Genesis 1:26-27, both male and female are created simultaneously in the image of God. Though in this account the woman appears more as an instrument by which the race can "increase and multiply," the older version makes clear the level of companionship which Adam sought and found in her.[9]

In either case, the Fall effects an overturning of the order of the universe, and one of the chief results is male domination of woman (Gen. 3:16). Thus the Biblical writer reasoned from the obviously inferior position of women in his society back to a time when things were quite different. But the implication was also drawn from the Genesis story that the state of inequality presently perceived was divinely and permanently willed; even in the Christian era, the power of baptism to call us to a new order of existence, transcending the curse, was not always granted. At best those women who had placed their sexuality under the internal and external controls of the vow of virginity were viewed as fairly redeemed, though the severity of the external controls hints how tenuous this redemption was thought to be—and how deeply the "original sin" was defined in terms of sexuality, despite the lack of evidence for this in the Genesis account in the first place. Even the people of the Kingdom were—and are—a long way from seeing themselves as "suitable helpmates." (Actually, in this context the word "helpmate" is redundant, both a corruption and an offshoot of help which is "meet" or "suitable." "Suitable help" was what Eve constituted for Adam by her very nature—and Adam for Eve, though the Biblical writers do not make this explicit.)

The notions of interdependence and support found in the "helpmate" image are powerful forces in the lives of many women, and they are not confined to marriage as modern usage of the word itself might tend to suggest. Insofar as Mary was "helpmate" to her son, she went beyond her mother role to be companion and friend. Insofar as she was "helpmate" to her people, she lived and acted with a consciousness of connectedness to a corporate body that gave resonance and wider meaning to her personal life. And insofar as she was "helpmate" to Joseph—a role so often forgotten—she embodied the relatedness of body, mind and heart that deepens and enriches the physical exchange of sexuality in marriage.

Perhaps the unusual priority which her identity and calling took over his, and the fact that it is easier in this instance to think of the man as helpmate rather than the woman, underlines our neglect of the mutuality of the image. We do not see it possible, or likely, to be much help to anyone simply by being one's own self. On a personal level, we look for more tangible forms of assistance, whether physical or psychological, and assume strangely that the one being helped is in a position of superiority. Joseph's role is reduced to an even more functional one than Eve's in the first Genesis account: he is there to legitimize Mary's childbearing in the eyes of the public, and to protect and support the young family. Neither his fathering capacities nor his unique personal companionship to Mary receive much attention. On a corporate level of help, again, we usually have a very specific form of assistance in mind, although on this level the one offering it is the superior one; those who cast themselves on the mercy of "Mary, help of Christians" do so because of their need and their lowliness.

The traditional association of Mary with mercy reminds us of how deeply this quality is connected in our minds with the feminine principle, and especially with the maternal instinct: a woman, it is commonly held, responds more with sympathy and compassion; her judgments are personal and on a feeling level; she is not interested in upholding an abstract order of law; she will forgive her children anything. To be helpful and supportive is her nature; a woman who is not kind is not only cruel, she is unnatural. Mary, we know, will understand and pity; we can get from, or through her, an absolution that we could not get from God.

The danger of such a dichotomy between love and justice has been noted by many students of mariology: if Mary was the representative of love, then God was confined to the sphere of justice, and by extension tended to become a rigid, impersonal, avenging figure whose punishments were stayed only by the pleading and intercession of his compassionate mother. Such an assignment of traits came naturally to a culture which tended to view its deity under anthropomorphic, male images. Had it been able to conceive of the transcendent being as beyond sexuality, encompassing both male and female qualities, this limitation upon the divine completeness of being could never have taken the hold that it did upon the popular imagination. And even more significantly, the impetus of divine sanction would have been applied not to acceptance and strengthening of the dichotomy on a human level, but to challenging it and supporting efforts at integration.

For love and justice are not opposites, though their caricatures may appear to be, and they are separated only at the cost of their vitality and authenticity. True justice is not rigid and impersonal; true love is not spinelessly compliant, nor devoid of objective content. Neither quality can be assigned to one sex rather than the other. And neither is properly appropriated to the public or private sphere alone: love must irradiate and humanize our public functioning; justice must suffuse our personal relationships. If our capacity for one quality seems more highly developed than the other, the odds are that we are over-rating our competence even in the developed area, let alone our completeness and unity of being.

All too often, the impulse to be helpful stems from a superficial level of a woman's personality, and expresses a vague and undirected sense of relatedness. The final, and one of the most crucial, tasks assigned to Psyche in her mythic struggle to be reunited with Eros, the god of love, entails a caution against just this characteristic feminine impulse. She is ordered to journey to the underworld to secure a special ointment from Persephone; en route, she is told, she must be sure to ignore requests for help from a series of figures in need—a lame donkey driver, a corpse floating by her boat in the river of the dead, some old weaving women, all of whom will beg her to stop. In other words, as Erich Neumann interprets the episode, the ego must focus itself decisively on its ultimate goal, and resist the distractions of relatedness, no matter how tempted it is by immediate needs and requests. Originally, among primitive people, Neumann points out, helping involved a participation mystique, a sense of identifying with the one helped, which could lead to possession by them, and so was not without its psychic dangers.[10]

The injunction against pity has the wisdom of paradox. Those who seek to express real love must discriminate it from sentimentality, raising to consciousness both their motives and the long-range implications of their actions. A certain tough, even hard-minded objectivity will anchor attempts to live a life of love in a healthy and realistic way, as Christian wisdom has long known; one thinks of Vincent de Paul's warning to the Daughters of Charity—"it is for your love alone that the poor will forgive you the bread you bring them." In our own time, we are coming to the awareness that struggling against the systemic causes of poverty and oppression will help the poor more in the long run than simply giving material aid. Working directly to alleviate suffering may be personally more satisfying; while it fills our need for approval and affiliation, however, it allows the roots of the problem to continue unchallenged. The poor will not forgive us the bread we bring them now, until we have empowered them to bake their own.

At the same time, the helpfulness of simple presence is a factor which cannot be ignored. In our struggle to "do something," whether on a personal or a systemic level, we underestimate what "being something" can do all by itself. By a mysterious principle of synchronicity, Jungians point out, those who are in a right relation to themselves call out a greater harmony or actual healing in their environment and those around them.[11] This is something different from the effect of a conscious prayer of petition, and goes beyond the power of good example or the freeing influence of "model-breakers" referred to in the Introduction; we understand so little of our unconscious power to receive and transmit psychic forces, whether positive or negative.

The ancient rainmaker stands as testimony to this. If he achieved within himself the right connection to the powers of the Beyond, the desired rain would fall. His presence was the quite unconscious catalyst; in Irene Claremont de Castillejo's words, he did not *cause* the rain to fall, he *allowed* it:

> The essence of the Rainmaker is that he knows how to allow. . . . In those rare moments when all the opposites meet within a man, good and also evil, light and also darkness, spirit and also body, brain and also heart, masculine focused consciousness and at the same time feminine diffuse awareness, wisdom of maturity and childlike wonder; when all are allowed and none displaces any other in the mind of a man, then that man, though he may utter no word, is in an attitude of prayer. Whether he knows it or not his own receptive allowing will affect all those around him.[12]

So too, George Maloney points out, Mary was a "rain-maker" for the people in her life, indeed, for her whole nation.[13] Her presence is noted in the Gospels more often than her words or actions—at Cana, on Calvary, in the upper room at Pentecost. By being there, she made things different—though in a different way each time. At Cana she is shown as enabling Christ to take a dramatic step of self-exposure and decisively begin his public ministry. On Calvary she could "do" nothing—rainmaking at its purest. In the upper room, she *was* in community with the other disciples in a way that she does not seem to have been before, the passage through suffering and failure to the total triumph of the risen Savior having united them in an utterly new way.

Now they shared not only memories but a living sense of a common principle of life and destiny. The more that Christ's divinity became real to the disciples, the more marvelous must have seemed to them the great mystery of the Incarnation—and the more strength and joy must they have found in her who stood among them as the living link of God and man. The Spirit moves us often through other human beings. Who is to say it was not her eyes that challenged them, her smile that encouraged them, or her words which impelled them to pull back the latch and move out into the sunshine of the Pentecost morning? Or was it simply her presence which told them they could not stay cooped up in that room hoarding the knowledge of his immense and passionate love of the human race, not letting it break through them, not really believing how much their lives had been penetrated by his, not, after all, knowing that they had been loved.

Without breaking the sense of simple equality and unity in their experience of prayer together, surely in some way she communicated how much the Spirit was to be trusted, how deeply his life lived on in theirs, how right it was to share it with the poor, the lonely, the crippled, the world outside that did not know. How just it was to love. For somehow, the tongues of fire rained down.

The Corporate Self

If a new corporate identity emerged for Mary on Pentecost, it was not the only corporate identity in her life. The truly radical nature of the Spirit's action within her and between her and the rest of the disciples can only be appreciated to the extent that we understand the prior claim that Judaism had upon her entire personality and self-understanding. She was "Daughter of Zion" in fact, whether or not the phrase is consciously applied to her in the Gospels;[14] she was the descendant and legitimate heir of Sarah, Rebecca, Rachel and Leah, as her father had prayed, though in a way he might not have foreseen.

Her foremothers wheel across the pages of the Old Testament, full of life and vitality, passion and purpose. The actual mothers are in some ways more interesting than the "nontraditional" heroines, Esther and Judith: for all their courage, these last are really instruments to fulfill the wishes of men, and use their beauty in a rather ambiguous, if not downright corrupt, way.

The mothers have all the single-minded, almost pitiless determination of the warrior or politician, plus a basic self-assertiveness and—at least in Sarah's case—a sense of humor that is not beyond laughing at and with the Lord God himself. Her laughter begins in amused skepticism and ends in delighted admiration over her late-born son Isaac ("God has laughed"). The Lord renames Sarah, as he does her husband, and affirms her totally, including what seems to have been a formidable temper; when she insists that her maidservant Hagar and son Ismael be cast out into the wilderness for mocking Isaac, God orders Abraham: "Grant Sarah all she asks of you" (Genesis 21:12).

Rebecca too is a decisive vehicle of the Lord's will. Her preferential love of her son Jacob and securing of his father's blessing for him are affirmed as correct by later salvation history, despite what seems a rather mean trick on Esau.[15] Here a mother judges between two of her own sons; her love "knows" who is the true inheritor of the Promise.

And though that inheritor, Jacob, himself chooses Rachel over her sister Leah for his wife, by another trick he is forced to marry Leah first; it is from her children that the house of David will spring and the Promise be carried on. Beautiful and strong-willed, Rachel endures not only sharing her husband with Leah, but watching her sister bear him seven children before she even bears him one. Her first-born, however, is Joseph, who will save all his brothers and through them the twelve tribes of Israel at the time of the famine; thus she too "mothers the Promise." Rivals for Jacob's love, Rachel and Leah ultimately join in supporting him against their own father, and approve his plan to return to his own homeland as the

Lord had commanded. Rachel even steals her father's household gods to bring with them, in what looks like an idolatrous impulse; it actually brings about an encounter and covenant of reconciliation between her husband and her father, and a parting with benediction and kisses instead of anger (Gen. 31:17-55).

Like another woman of Genesis, perhaps, she is "looking back" toward the only home she has known. But rather than being turned into a pillar of salt, Rachel successfully follows through in her journey. Or rather, literally, she "sits on" the household gods, symbols of her local identity and ancestral spirits, until past and future, local and universal, are integrated, in the reconciliation of father and husband. How typical a patriarchal interpretation it is to make Lot's wife a symbol of disobedience or idle female curiosity. The symbol-readers do not usually point out what is very clear from the entire story in Genesis: that Lot himself is basically weak and doubtful about his own ability to leave the doomed city or to reach the hill-country. Before his escape, he is shown as preferring to expose his daughters to the depraved townspeople of Sodom, rather than his male guests who are actually angelic messengers. It is small wonder that his wife cannot look ahead with hope or courage and becomes paralyzed, caught between past and future, the known and the unknown (Gen. 19:1-29). "Helpmating" works both ways, or it does not work at all.

As Rachel knew she must somehow incorporate her past and the memory of her ancestors into her new life,[16] so Mary would have reverenced and pondered *her* ancestors. The more she felt the newness of her call, the more she would have looked back and tried to see the essential connecting threads, cutting away the accidentals until the line of God's fidelity and love stood out, embodied as it was in all the various personalities and twists of history.

Sarah and Rebecca, Rachel and Leah, would have comforted her, for they would have told her how far beyond their own dreams, and yet how very much through their own individual human nature, God's love had carried them. Women closer to her in history would have said the same: Ruth, whose presentation of herself to Boaz as his handmaid is echoed in Mary's fiat;[17] Hannah, whose song of delight at her childbearing (1 Sam. 2:1-11) sounds so much like the Magnificat; the mother of the Machabees, who precedes Mary in "disowning" her sons and thereby encouraging them to assume their full, free identity before God:

> I do not know how you appeared in my womb; it was not I who endowed you with breath and life, I had not the shaping of your every part. It is the creator of the world, ordaining the process of man's birth and presiding over the origin of all things, who in his mercy will most surely give you back both breath and life, seeing that you now despise your own existence for the sake of his laws. (2 Mach. 7:22-23).[18]

Parts of herself could identify with all these women, each so very different from the other, all so much a part of the Promise, not only by the sons they mothered but by their own living relationship to the Lord, and presence among their people.

Relatedness was a central fact of Jewish life on both a vertical and a horizontal level; a Jewish man or woman was a member of a family, tribe and nation at the same time.[19] The strong corporate identity of the Jewish people would have played an intimate role in Mary's concept of herself, as in that of every member of her race. Together, through their common father, Abraham, they had received the Promise; together they had come out of Egypt, wandered in the desert, found and entered the Promised Land. Together they had betrayed the Lord, repented and returned; in spite of all their historical ups and downs, the seeds of their own salvation were within them. Together, they awaited the Messiah.

"Because he is the one who is to save his people from their sins" (Matt. 1:21). How much strength she would derive, at the time of the Annunciation, from the thought of what it would mean for her people—his people. Whatever Mary's understanding of the Kingdom, it must have included expectation of the redress of the social and economic inequities she saw around her, a lightening of the yoke under which the poor labored so patiently while the powerful surrounded themselves with luxury. In between palace intrigues and murder of his rivals, Herod the Great was lavishing money on building projects, temples, theatres, fortresses. As a devout Jew, Mary would have been aware that profit-making and harsh indifference to the burdens of the common man had encroached even on sacred territory and religious institutions. Elizabeth and Zachary, who were of the priestly class, could have added to her knowledge of religious injustice and the need for reform, to which their own son would later speak so forcefully.

One young girl could hardly have done much about the pervasive corruption, except to name it in her heart and live against it: Widows scraped to the bottom of their savings to pay their mite; farmers worried about the weather and the soil; fisherman and shepherds worked through the night to support their families; marginal people, the old, beggars, cripples, lepers, the mentally ill or possessed, lived on wearily and without hope. Foreign invaders wielded power; those who cooperated rose in influence, while others plotted violent revolution. Her people had the Promised Land back, if on uneasy terms with the Roman occupiers; they were also on uneasy terms within themselves.

Among them waited an element with especially clear memories and values: the *anawim* or faithful poor. These were the "remnant," who had returned to Jerusalem after the exile, and still looked with expectation toward the coming of the Messiah; they were able to interpret the confusion and pain of the present in the light of the promised redemption, trusting themselves to the Lord rather than to worldly power or accomplishment. In the Old Testament, they are often referred to collectively as the "Daughter of Zion." The lamps of their faith were kept burning; their eyes were on the hands of their master. They would be ready when he came.

Mary was clearly of this group. The memory of her forebears and the knowledge of the needs of God's chosen people in the present converged in her. She was one who could still hear the voice of the Lord, and connect it to the reality of Jewish life. When she spoke her fiat, it was for all the Jewish nation, as the angel had predicted—and in effect, for all the human race, even those who did not know there was something worth waiting for.

In doing so, she was following in the line of her male as well as female ancestors. We confine Mary most unfairly if we only look at the feminine role models given her by the Judaic tradition. Luke's Gospel presents the Annunciation scene in terms which link it to the vocation of many Old Testament leaders—that is, as a direct call to a momentous mission, with assurance that God will be with the person in all difficulties, enabling him to accomplish the task if he accepts it. So the history of Israel was seen to depend on the response of Isaac (Gen. 26:24); Jacob (Gen. 28:15-20); Gideon (Jdg. 6:16); Jeremiah (1:8); so it now depended on one woman, who personified her nation.[20] Similarly, the Magnificat brings out the analogy which best expresses the importance of Mary's role to the Jewish race: her similarity to Abraham, the father of believers, who is the source of blessing for, and will be blessed by, all nations.[21]

Before God, either male or female could stand for the race and speak for it. Abraham's consent began the Covenant; Mary's consent fulfilled it.

The Just Woman

Though the Gospel takes care to note that Joseph was a "just man," we do not often speak of the justice of Mary. Mercy seems to us her forte, justice an inferior quality, or at least one of lesser importance. Later in her cult, she will be seen as the perennial recourse of those who are "outlawed"—robbers, murderers, those who have sold their souls to the devil— overturning the decisions of the Trinity and throwing the court of heaven into chaos. In this, she is embodying the popular imagination's view of the feminine approach to reality, as has been pointed out. Because of the subjective and personal character of a woman's judgments, it is commonly suspected, she is simply not well equipped to "do justice." As long as a male-constructed system of law and order can control society, it seems an unimportant, even endearing failure in her. And yet in the Jewish Kabbala, justice is on the left or feminine side of the Sephiroth tree, and in mythology feminine figures such as the Furies, Nemesis and the Fates administer justice at a level so profound not even Zeus is superior to it.[22] Astraea, the virgin daughter of Justice, was last of all the gods and goddesses to leave the earth at the end of the Golden Age.[23]

The depths of justice are not always susceptible to

rational analysis, brave and impressive as are man's attempts to codify and order them in a comprehensible way. Neither can law be applied across-the-board with arithmetical neatness and without attention to individual situations; the principle of equity has long-standing acceptance, with its modification of pretensions to universal, objective judgment. In its origins and in its application, justice is hardly a specifically masculine talent.

Nor are social structures fool-proof mediators of justice, no matter how high the ideals on which they were founded. Holding back barbarism and chaos, they are still all too likely to institutionalize double standards of treatment based on economic and racial differences. In Mary's time as in our own, those who "hungered and thirsted for justice" did so despite the existence of an elaborate code of law and judicial system.

The Magnificat stands as a climactic enunciation of the passionate commitment of the Jewish people to the ultimate "doing of justice" by the Messiah: wrongs will be righted, imbalance corrected, the poor and lowly raised again to human dignity. Whether the hymn is to be credited to Mary or not, it is significant that the early Christian community felt it to be an appropriate expression of her attitude toward the Incarnation, with its focus on the social and political, rather than the personal and maternal.

Her own approach to justice is implicit, though very undeveloped, in the Gospel narratives. Her care in observing both civil and religious law has often been noted, as in the journey to Bethlehem to be counted in the census, the fulfilling of the rites of circumcision and presentation of her child in the Temple, or the festival journeys to Jerusalem. On the level of personal relationship, the dilemma which she and Joseph faced with regard to their marriage after the Annunciation certainly involved a real pondering of their debt to each other and to God, perhaps with the laws of defilement as a basis.[24] As parents, again, they held and exercised authority over their son, who was subject to them: the enacting of justice requires that we assume our rightful authority and speak from it, while remaining open to the possibilities of change and development and—strikingly re-emphasized in the scene of their reunion with their "runaway son" in the Temple—the mysterious imperatives of the Father's will. True justice, like love, presupposes a firmly-established ego identity and a sense of self-respect; but it does not eliminate the need to search, to discern, to revise expectations, or to live with mystery—the relative otherness of human freedom and personal vocation, the absolute otherness of the transcendent.

At the same time, "mystery" can become an excuse for failure to act, a fog that clouds our judgment and sanctions acceptance of quite human, though complex and long-standing, error. What must be, must be, we say—it's the way things are. "Mystery" never was this for Jesus. His human life was a thoroughly consistent, measured but passionate drive "towards Jerusalem"—toward the city of the Temple, the lawful center of Judaism, and the spokesmen and leaders of his Father's people. His own powerful hunger and thirst for justice orders his dealings with everyone whom he meets along the way, man, woman, Pharisee, Sadducee, Samaritan, Greek. He speaks with authority, and listens with it; he calls together and instructs a group who will extend his efforts through time and space; his own messianic mission springs totally from who he is and must be by the Father's will. Not knowing himself the time for the reestablishment of the Kingdom (Mk. 13:32), he knows his own hour when it comes and goes to meet it. "Mystery" here generates clear vision and wholehearted action, because it springs not from an arbitrary Oriental despot, but from a Being who transcends all human authority, male or female, a Being who *is* Justice.

Insofar as she too was totally open and given to this transcendent God and lived out her singular call to messianic motherhood, Mary too embodied the search for justice as much as any human being can. Her face too was "set toward Jerusalem"; every one of her recorded actions in the Gospel describes the practice of a believing Jewish woman. She knew her religion, and its leaders. Every moment of Christ's public ministry, every word of challenge from his lips, every confrontation with the Pharisees, must have given her a clearer sense of what "her hour" would be—and where.

Calvary may have shocked, but it could not have surprised her. It had been clear for many months that her son was a sign that would be contradicted, and contradicted forcefully and cleverly at the highest levels of human power. It may have crossed her mind that she too was in danger; the execution of women for political reasons was not unheard of.[25] "Doing justice," no doubt, along the way, treating those she met with dignity and respect as human beings, and fulfilling the law of holyday observance, she went up to Jerusalem once more for the Passover feast, and found her hour had come.

The carefully constructed symbolism of John's Gospel throws this into sharp relief.[26] For Mary, standing on Calvary was a political act—one done out of the most natural and deepest of personal human instincts, done unthinkingly perhaps, without ever dreaming of having had any choice in the matter—but a political act all the same. By her silent presence she identifies and passively resists an injustice so great that human words could not begin to describe it. If the Greek Furies were driven to vengeance by an act of parricide committed outside of the law, what were the furies unleashed within her by an act of deicide committed by the representatives of the law itself? And what singular understanding of the mysterious depths of transcendent justice led her to continue standing there?

John, who is the only evangelist to represent her as actually present at the scene, asks us by his description to believe that she and the women with her had come to terms with transcendence in the midst of deepest pain. Divine justice is that out of which human justice comes, and to which—sometimes limping badly—it returns. This justice clarifies our choices, if we let it, helping us to know what it is we must do, leading us not to settle for less, nor to strive for more. It is a justice acquainted with long-range processes and the slow swing of time, the heaping up of historical complications, and conscious and unconscious violations of nature and human obligation. It is well aware of how nature can avenge herself, how many crimes create their own punishment.[27] Still, it calls on us to take part in a line of development that we do not fully understand, to collaborate in processes which we did not begin and which cannot be finished in our lifetime. We may "take the law into our own hands"—sometimes with unfortunate consequences—but we cannot do the same with justice; it is larger than we. What we must do is put our hands on it, that portion of it which we are allowed to touch and realize with the time given us. That is our imperative, the mandate of our individual and collective "hour."

Time was telescoped on Calvary, human history recapitulated and redeemed. In taking her stand, Mary witnessed to the absolute uncategorical innocence of the victim, the incomprehensible evil which brought his death, and the power of the still more incomprehensible divine will which accepted it. She "put her hand on" a greater portion of the arch of justice than anyone before had ever touched—because she saw with her devastated mother's heart how much was included in this one event, how deeply the Old Law had been fulfilled and superseded, how closely, in the end, justice was connected with love.

Her "hour," the justice-doing toward which she had been journeying her whole life long, was this very active realization and testimony. She who represented Judaism at its purest and best now imperceptibly became the representative of a new order.

In primitive Germanic societies, the daughters of kings were often called "peace-weavers," for they were given in marriage to the kings of hostile nations in order to bring about an end to conflict. We could well call Mary a justice-weaver, as with all her memories of Abraham and Sarah, Rebecca and Isaac, Rachel, Leah and Jacob, she turned toward the Christian community, and the men and women who would find life together in the risen Christ, from her hour until the end of human history. But no one had to "give her" to this work; it happened within her pondering heart. Christ recognized and externalized it with his words to her and John—taking their eyes from him for an instant, as he seemed to want, they looked at each other and the future. And in their mutual care for one another, the new Church was already forming.

The Related Self

In all that has been said, it should be clear that Mary entered into life and relationship creatively. While we do not have enough information to be much more specific, it seems that her relationship with

Christ and his disciples was one of freedom and support—the healthy kind of polarity which Ann Ulanov
sees as part of the original structure of grace. Such
polarity is opposed, both within and among in-
dividuals, to an unhealthy polarization of masculine
and feminine:

> In polarity, the opposites are related to each
> other by mutual attraction; they are drawn to
> unite with each other without destroying the
> distinct individuality of each pole; on the con-
> trary, the individuality of each is heightened and
> realized.[28]

In polarization, on the other hand, the relationship
has caved in, and the opposites struggle for
dominance:

> Instead of each person living his own distinct
> sexuality and blend of male and female psychic
> factors, each sex now clashes with the other and
> each exacerbates the negative expression of the
> other. . . . Each feels the other does not and
> cannot understand his point of view because he
> is so fundamentally different.[29]

In such a state, people often relate to each other
through the roles that they play, rather than from the
heart; the maternal role is one frequently adopted,
since it receives so much collective encouragement in
our culture as *the* feminine role par excellence. But
the woman who throws her heart and soul into playing it "often ends up feeling like hired help, plundered

of her deepest hopes of service," while in polarity, basically, "there are no roles to play; there is only the relation of person to person. That is central, the rest is merely peripheral. When this center is maintained, all else falls into place and revolves around it."[30]

It hardly seems likely that Christ would have wished upon his Church a mother who specialized in producing guilt by her compulsive filling of the maternal role, or by her constant reminder to one and all of her superior nobility and generosity. The more desirable—and more probable—gift he willed us was a woman who related to his Father and to him simply from the heart, playing no compulsive role, but being herself as honestly and totally as she knew how. Such a polarity does not assume that the other is so "fundamentally different" that there is no basis for communication or understanding, or that predetermined traditional roles are the only channel through which communication can take place; neither does it over-identify with the other to the point that all differences are erased, and all potential for surprise and growth as well.

The polarity of person to person, whether in prayer, in individual human relationships, or in community, is a delicate balance, and a dynamic one—a dance, if you will, with constantly changing rhythms and movements. It always runs the risk of falling back into something fixed and rigid—a standstill—or a solo performance where one partner dominates to the point that the other is reduced to a permanently passive bystander. There is always the possibility that one partner may forget, or fail to attend to, the dance within at the same time—the unique interplay of masculine and feminine factors in every human personality, and in the godhead itself. Those who hold up Mary to us as a model of the feminine stance which every soul, male or female, should adopt in prayer, may be prescribing something badly needed by men today; but it may not be all that is needed by women or by society. And it does run the risk of turning the transcendent back into the masculine category, i.e., into an incomplete realization of its richness.

God speaks, and we speak. Contemplatives know the fruitfulness of being "feminine," of letting go, surrendering, giving the transcendent space to speak and act, allowing it to possess us. But who is so feminine as God, sometimes, so patient, waiting, faithfully and silently, giving us so much space, wanting to hear what we will say, looking to see what we will do?

The rhythm and complementarity of life within the Trinity extend outwards; our "dance with God," in turn, offers us a pattern for human relationships that are flexible, resilient, richly mutual. And human love and justice, with their profound transformation of our personalities, mirror back the truth that in the end all roles will drop away. At that point, though we may only know it sporadically and for brief moments now, being and doing, giving and receiving, body and spirit, "the fire and the rose" will be one.

This is the faith which enables us now to play the role that the "dance of the Christian community" calls us to—to mother and father and sister and brother one another in Christ, which is, in effect (Mk. 3:35), to do the will of God.

* * *

One-in-herself, Mary was also part of a family, a society, and in the later years of her life, a new community. More than most of us, perhaps, she had a need for clear-headedness in her relationships, and for the courage which enabled her to act out of a value system not always understood by her friends and relatives. But it was a value system which included care and concern for others at its core. She had great need, too, for genuine feeling for people who did not see things her way, to whom she could not express half of what was in her heart, people who had to be warmed into forgiving her for the revolutionary bread she brought them—made to see, somehow, that it was their bread, not simply hers, and that this mother had borne life which would transform them, and the very cosmos.

Chapter Three
Living Symbol

We live and die, some few of us having been "legends in our own time," most of us, not. Time plays tricks with the memory we leave behind us anyway: most of us, again, are wiped out of human consciousness altogether; what energy and admiration we might have drawn to ourselves are gathered instead to a few mythic figures, who for one reason or another fill the need of an age or a race to believe and revere. Not that the object of the myth-making process needs to be world-renowned. Church records are filled with local saints; indeed, in ancient times the state of sanctity was ascertained by popular acclaim, and when ceremonies for it were formalized, canonization took place in the new saint's own district, after investigation by the local bishop. And every family or community has its ancestral spirits, about whom stories are passed down through the generations.

Mythologizing the achievements and stature of other human beings is a universal human tendency, for better or worse. There is something generous and expansive about admiration; giving it helps to anchor our sense of what we value most and makes us believe more in our own human potential for good, or at any rate for endurance. A world without heroes is a world without values, and/or hope.

107

The coin of course has another side. Mythologizing can run reality into the ground; we can hold up heroes so removed from the facts of their lives as to invite skepticism, so idealized as to cause us to lose interest, for the gap between them and us is so wide we can hardly see them, let alone pattern ourselves after them. Or they can pull us into an unreal world, enabling us to escape living in the here and now; the ties that bind beyond the grave, if not properly understood, cut deeply into our capacity to love in the present life, and to grow in our own way to our own truth.

For Christians the mysterious identity of the historical and the mystical Christ holds a key to the problem of initiation and development. Guided by the Gospel in growing to maturity individually and as a community, we believe we are also growing, slowly, into Christ. "I live now," writes Paul, "not with my own life but with the life of Christ who lives in me" (Gal. 2:20). He is going through labor pains, that the Galatians too may be born in Christ (Gal. 3:19), and counsels the Ephesians to work together in unity, building up the body of Christ, until they become "fully mature with the fullness of Christ himself" (Eph. 4:12-13). The Church which is one with the mystical Christ grows and develops throughout history, carrying with it and expressing anew in every age the fundamental identity of its founder, discovering more and more not merely the myth, but the dynamic reality of his being. Human history is not cancelled out, but given its true significance; we are getting not farther and farther away from the hero, but closer and closer to him.

If there is a seamless unity between the historical and the mystical Christ, however, we have no guarantee that such a unity exists between the historical and the "mystical" Mary. In fact, because so very little is known of the historical Mary, the "mystical" one was freed to float through history, regarded and portrayed not in basic relationship to the living person but in relation to the needs and desires of her devotees in every age. Whether or not we are getting closer to the first Christian woman is a matter of some doubt.

The problematic nature of knowledge of Mary is compounded by the thoroughly masculine character of Christian symbolism of the deity, and the largely masculine constitution of the official structures of the Christian churches. The result of this onesidedness on so many levels has been to place the burden of compensating for it directly on her: Mary stands for the feminine in Christianity. Carrying the weight of this symbolic function, she has at times been lifted out of her rightful position at the center of the communion of saints, and made an unofficial fourth member of the Trinity, as a universal archetype of the feminine. Thus Carl Jung reads the Assumption, as recognition of the divinized status of all that had for so long been denigrated in the patriarchal Judaeo-Christian religion, and absolutely excluded from Protestant forms of that tradition.[1] But to become the incarnation of an archetypal idea of this stature almost automatically involves a restructuring of reality, and a sizable degree of remoteness from the individual self. Neither Christ nor any of the Twelve was ever made to function for "the masculine" to the extent which Mary has been seen to function for "the feminine." I am "tired of the gender of things," Anne Sexton grumbles, "I'm no more a woman than Christ was a man."[2] The Virgin might legitimately have the same complaint.

Actually, gender itself is not the only thing at stake in the history of Marian symbolism. Though held up as embodying the feminine, Mary is really only shown to represent one aspect of it, the good or positive side of the principle. Officially, she lacks a "shadow," the dark side of the feminine archetype, and it is surely no accident that periods when her cult has particularly flourished have also experienced the rise of counter-figures who seem only to embody this darker side—shrews and witches. A neglected aspect will always take its revenge, as Marie-Louise von Franz points out; payment will be exacted in time.[3]

The Marian cult may not tell us very much about the original woman, but it does tell us a great deal about ourselves. Indeed, the relatively conservative and spare quality of officially sanctioned Marian dogma was no match for the tide of popular imagination, as it rushed in to claim her for its own. And even the doctrinal pronouncements and patristic writings can be shown to be conditioned by definite, limited world views and calculated to meet social, political and psychological needs of the time, as much as they seek to express universal truth. The contradictions between the "official Mary" and the "people's Mary" could be viewed as a self-perpetuating cycle of compensation and reaction, as could the various local and national Marian theologies that have evolved, and that caused such tension among representatives at the second Vatican Council. Careful compromise and selectivity marked the final official formulations in the Council's Constitution on the Church. In turn, the "people's Mary" has been slow to endorse any of the Council documents; "Our Lady of Bayside," for one, has been downright critical.

Myth, however, can do more than meet broadly political purposes or serve as an emotional outlet for the powerless. It ought also to be acknowledged, at least potentially, as one of the most politically inconvenient and profound vehicles of truth within human experience. In its persistence and its ability to communicate on levels inaccessible to strictly rational thought or language, it can be a very healthy challenge to the "body politic," if at times a suspect one—witness the banishment of poets from Plato's Republic. Only a foolhardy group, whether of scholars, bishops or philosopher-kings, would choose to take the emotional hungers of the human race today lightly, let alone those of the human race throughout history.

Myth, moreover, is a way of explaining and transmitting religious belief. Even in Scripture we are already dealing with Mary largely from a symbolic point of view, as the evangelists selected and patterned episodes involving her to express aspects of their faith experience. Having been left largely with symbol, modern biblical scholarship has pointed out, we have been left with something of value after all, though a different kind of value from history. Read with discrimination and sensitivity, the story of Mary, the mystical symbol, is an important part of the story of Christianity, and of ourselves; mariology and ecclesiology still go hand in hand and illuminate one another, as they have from ancient times.

The "mystical" Mary and the Church, in fact, can be seen to call one another on in pursuit of the full measure of Christian identity. What a Church it would be if it were truly like the Mary we image to ourselves: sensitive, approachable, alert and responsive to human suffering, warmly interested in human beings and understanding of their weaknesses, mediating to them the divine love which she has experienced in her heart. What a Mary *she* would be if she were truly like the ecclesial community of which we dream— alive and dynamic, listening to and acting bravely on the voice of the Spirit, facing into the future, not frozen on a pedestal like a statue for whom there is no question of further growth.

That this is *not* our primary image of her is not her fault, of course. It is something that we have done to her, an impoverishment caused by our static understanding of holiness and of life—and also by our static understanding of the feminine, with which we have so closely associated her.

Static Symbolism

The positive side of the feminine principle in particular, the very one which Mary is seen as embodying, is vulnerable to such a static approach, because its nature has an inert and unchanging quality. It does not initiate, but conserves and shelters; stability is essential to it. The dark, receptive, enclosing world of the maternal womb expresses its basic character as a vessel. The feminine body is a natural symbol of the original psychic situation of the human race, the undifferentiated unity of man and world in the Great Round, which is also symbolized by the circular snake or the uroboros. As the world was experienced by man as a great vault or vessel which encompassed and generated life, so woman's body was experienced as the "life-vessel," identified with matter and with the world. Erich Neumann identifies the resulting symbolic formula as basic to the matriarchal stage of consciousness: "woman = body = vessel = world."[4]

Other symbolic manifestations of the elementary feminine vessel, according to Neumann, would be the "wombs" of the earth—subterranean darkness, chasms, caves, abysses, valleys, rocks and mountains—and containers such as boxes, baskets, chests, coffins, tombs, nests, cradles, beds, ships, wagons. The sheltering aspects of the cave are extended culturally in constructions such as a temple, house, village, city, fence or wall.

The womb is not simply a container, however, but a nourisher and transformer as well, and so can express more than stasis. There is a dynamic side to the feminine principle, associated with birth, rebirth, inspiration, and creativity. Feminine vessel symbols which accent the possibilities of transformation—jar, kettle, oven, retort—or nourishment—bowl, goblet, chalice, grail—presuppose containment and build upon it. Other symbols have a further ambivalence: insofar as water is still and containing, as in ponds, lakes and wells, the "waters of the womb," it is feminine, although when flowing it participates in the fructifying and moving power of the masculine principle. Trees and other vegetation likewise can be seen in either light,[5] but they do have an inseparable matriarchal content: the Great Earth Mother is preeminently the mother of vegetation, the fertile bearer of fruit.

On both natural and human levels, it is of the essence of the mother to "be there," and by her sheltering presence to contain and nurture life.

The power of this primordial feminine principle was met with suspicious challenge by the patriarchal stage of consciousness, and especially by the Judaeo-Christian religion. The early Fathers treated Mary's title and prerogatives as "Mother of God" quite gingerly, in view of the still-flourishing cults of pagan goddesses. The notion of Mary as *our* mother developed a good deal later; according to Rene Laurentin,

Christians only began to consider her in this light in the 9th or 10th century, and even one of her most ardent advocates in the 12th century, Bernard of Clairvaux, does not make use of the image, regarding her rather as his queen.[6]

But whether motherhood is explicitly acknowledged or not, how much of Marian devotion is predicated on Mary's receptive presence, her "being there," so that humanity can go to her in time of need. A primitive Greek form of the *Sub tuum praesidium* dates from the 3rd or 4th century, and the prayer itself still rings on 20th century lips: "We fly to your protection, O Virgin Mother of God."[7] Bernard's own famous "look to the star" passage is just one of many examples that might be mentioned of Mary's perpetual availability; the disastrous motion and turbulence of the sinner are rhetorically contrasted with the serene stillness of the Virgin:

> If you will not be submerged by tempests, do not turn away your eyes from the splendour of this star! If the storms of temptations arise, if you crash against the rocks of tribulation, look to the star, call upon Mary. If you are tossed about on the waves of pride, of ambition, of slander, of hostility, look to the star, call upon Mary. . .[8]

For many other Western writers, Mary *is* Mother of Mercy without any qualification—"our life, our sweetness and our hope," as the *Salve Regina* called her. A new tenderness and humanity mark portrayals of her as the gentle, nurturing mother, both in literature and in art in the medieval period—very probably, as Hilda Graef postulates, the deliberate creation of a civilizing influence on the still primitive, barbarian Germanic tribes.[9]

A more hieratic image is typical of early Byzantine madonnas: theirs is the powerful Theotokos, Mother of God, the much-debated title awarded Mary at the Council of Ephesus in 431 A.D. Even later, in the 9th century, the Byzantine figure will be majestic rather than tender, her expression imperturbable and remote.[10] And yet for the crowds who hailed the Council's decision in the streets of 5th-century Ephesus, the issue of her right to the title of divine maternity was a highly emotional one, as emotional as the cult of Diana had been for them four hundred years earlier (cf. Acts 19:23-41). To the Council fathers, the Theotokos controversy was essentially Christological, of crucial importance because it called into question the unity of the divine and human natures of Christ; to the people outside, its significance may well have been seen differently.

Despite its difference in tone, Byzantine preaching on the Theotokos also partakes of the traditional feminine imagery of enclosed space and inert vessel. George Maloney has pointed out how much the Eastern fathers were given to calling Mary the Uroboros, the "womb of God."[11] To Proclus, she is the bridal chamber in which the Word espoused the flesh;[12] to Cyril, patriarch of Alexandria, she is the "never-extinguished lamp," the "never-destroyed sanctuary," the "vessel of the Incomprehensible."[13] Hesychius of

Jerusalem calls her the oven in which the offering for Yahweh was baked, "because an oven receives bread and fire from above, as also the Theotokos received the bread of life, that is the Word of God, and the fire of the presence of the Spirit into her womb."[14]

Certain Biblical images also offered themselves to development along the lines of the primordial feminine, among them the Ark of the Covenant and the "hortus conclusis," the enclosed garden of the Canticles. Both Eastern and Western writers avail themselves of these possibilities, although it was the Church *per se* which was originally the object of their comparisons. The application to Mary came somewhat later in time, underlining as it did the increasing tendency to see her and the Church in interchangeable terms.

Scripture scholars disagree as to whether or not Luke intended to create a parallel between Mary and the Ark of the Covenant in his infancy narrative. Those who believe affirmatively cite the use of the word "to overshadow," which is also applied to the *Shekinah,* the cloud symbolizing the divine presence, which filled the tabernacle in Exodus 40:35; in addition, they parallel Elizabeth's greeting of Mary at the Visitation with David's question in 2 Samuel 6:9: "How can the ark of the Lord come to me?"[15]

Whether the Ark parallel was deliberate or not, the concept of Mary as the dwelling place of God was picked up frequently in the patristic age. "Mary was the temple of God," writes Ambrose in his treatise on the Holy Spirit, "not the God of the temple." He is concerned that she be situated properly in the context of the divine plan: only the One who operated in the Temple is to be adored (III. 11. 80), and each Christian is a temple in which the Spirit also dwells (III. 12.90).[16] In the East, Leo VI turns the image around, contrasting rather than comparing Mary to the Ark itself: whereas the Ark was often in danger and liable to capture, she is a powerful, never-failing source of help.[17] She is addressed as the Ark again in the 7th-century Byzantine *Akathistos,* —the Ark "gilded by the Holy Spirit"—and in the Western litany of Loreto, which dates at least from the 12th century, although only standardized after the Reformation.[18] The more conventionalized the comparison becomes, the more it seems to address the inert, elementary character of the feminine, rather than its dynamic and transforming aspects. The divine indwelling, Christ had predicted to the Samaritan woman at the well, would one day transcend the Temple, and human persons would worship God "in spirit and in truth" (John 4:23). Still the human imagination clung to the protective vessel, the proven receptacle, the "still place" where God was known to have been.

In an equally popular image for much of the Christian era, Mary was pictured as the earth—the virgin territory which bore fruit through divine love. "God's Eden," Ephrem the Syrian calls her: the new garden, replacing the one lost through the willfulness of the first Eve. To Theodotus of Ancyra, she is the "unsown earth" which flowered forth the saving fruit and so surpassed Eden's garden of delights.[19] The earth imagery clustered more and more as time went on around the praise from Canticles 4:12: "She is a garden enclosed, my sister, my promised bride; a garden enclosed, a fountain sealed." In its fertility and its directedness, St. Jerome applied the image to Mary, as did many after him: "Because it is enclosed and sealed, it has a likeness to the Mother of the Lord."[20] It was one of her most familiar images in the Middle Ages, frequently depicted in the Hours of the Virgin, and also in the famed unicorn tapestries, where Mary sits in the center of the garden, while the unicorn (Christ) lays his paws in her lap.[21]

The theme of Mary as the enclosed garden lasted well into the seventeenth century, when it found its way into the allegorical pictures of the Jesuit emblem books. One such devotional piece, the *Partheneia Sacra* of Henry Hawkins, speaks of the Mary-garden as a place of perpetual spring, where grow all things needful to spiritual healing and comfort, and where only the "subtile wind" of the Holy Spirit can enter: "As th'Earth brought forth at first, how't is not knowne / So did this Garden, which was never sowne."[22]

Mary, then, is the marvelous vessel of God; both as a person and as the bearer of Christ, she is "full of grace," and the "fruit of her womb" is blessed. "Spiritual vessel," runs the litany of Loreto, "vessel of honor, singular vessel of devotion, tower of David, tower of ivory, house of gold . . . " Her inner space harbored the miracle of the Incarnation, and the

human imagination could not let drop the paradox of
the creator of the world enclosed within one of His
creatures.

There are, in addition, other images associated with
Mary that are less directly related to the vessel archetype, although they are all images of divine in-
strumentality and receptive, life-supporting presence.
Some of them are deeply rooted in Scripture, for example, Jacob's ladder, the cloud and the pillar of fire
that guided the Israelites in the desert, the fleece upon
which the dew of heaven descended (Jdg. 6:36-40),
or the burning bush on Mount Horeb (Exodus 3:2), a
symbol of her virginal love for God: it gave off light
while remaining unconsumed.[23] Others are more ex-
travagantly allegorical, and quite foreign to modern
taste. Beginning in the twelfth century, the concept of
Mary's intermediate position between Christ and his
body, the Church, causes her to be addressed as the
"neck of the Church" (cf. Cant. 4:4; 5:7, "thy neck is
like the tower of David, . . . a tower of ivory," and
the Pauline development of the idea of the Mystical
Body).

In a close alternate, for Bernard of Clairvaux, Mary
is an aqueduct, through which the divine waters of
grace can flow to earth.[24] Bernard, who is quite
capable of approaching God directly, presents Mary
as a human mediator of whom no one need be afraid,
and one especially helpful to the weak and timid, who
find a direct approach to God difficult. The linear and
hierarchical implications of such imagery and the concept of grace which they might be seen to imply, will

lead in time to the impasse over Mary as "mediatrix of all grace," and a narrow, shrewd spirituality which tries to manipulate the Godhead through cultivating her favors. Even imagery which has dynamic potential settles back into a fixed and static form, and the intermediate channel becomes a reservoir.

For all its potential for grasping, devouring and stagnating, it is the primordial feminine which has "staying power," at least in the popular imagination. The 14th and 15th century figures of the "Vierge Ouvrante" present Mary's triumphant though heretical secret: the body of the simple, traditional Madonna can be opened out to reveal the entire heavenly court, the Trinity, prophets, patriarchs and apostles, and/or the events of Christ's life, enclosed within her womb. The dynamism lies simply in swinging the closed "gate" open and perceiving what she embodies: life, past, present and future, birth and rebirth, the eternal reality behind the veil of the external, the temporal, the historical.[25] Depending on how we do this, we are either at stage one of human consciousness, the undifferentiated maternal uroboros (Marina Warner calls the figure fetish-like), or stage four, in which the psychic opposites have been consciously reconciled, and their unity flowers in a new collective identity between self, world and God.

Dynamic Symbolism

For the mystical Mary also owes a dimension of her being to the dynamic or transformative side of the feminine principle, and though it is less characteristic of orthodox religion to take note of this, it remains nevertheless a powerful factor in her female identity.

The transformations which take place in the maternal vessel allow spirit to come into being slowly, quietly, without severing its bonds from its native soil. This is unlike transformations worked by the masculine archetype, which are sudden and have the quality of a surprise attack, characteristically symbolized by lightning.[26] The characteristic symbol of feminine spiritual transformation, on the other hand, is the moon.

The transformative effects of the feminine principle have both a positive and a negative side. Positively, the dynamic feminine calls one out of oneself in a creative way, and impels openness to new insights or relationships, with hope in the future and the end result of the process, even at times with ecstasy. Negatively, it can lead to confusion, drunkenness, obsessive states, dissolution of the protective boundary between the rational and the irrational.[27] The connection of the full moon with "lunacy" is commonplace, as is the cognate relationship between *uterus* (womb) and *hyster* (hysterical).

In patriarchal mythologies, the significance of lunar or matriarchal consciousness is devalued and seen as secondary and derivative, "less pure" than that of the incorporeal sun, which is identified as the realm of "pure spirit." The profound influence of the moon on the earth, its tidal flow and fertility became evidence of its "earth-bound" and therefore inferior state. The scientific fact that the moon reflects the light of the sun, which man discovered comparatively late in time, confirmed his judgment and cemented the dominance of patriarchal "solar" consciousness.[28] It is as Selene, the ancillary and lesser light, that patristic writers first speak of the Church, and then of Mary, both receiving their power to shine from their connection with the Christian sun/Son of justice. Humbly receiving and absorbing the solar light, their rhythms and phases mysteriously but faithfully govern the engendering of life on earth, and bear testimony to the divine will to work with humanity as a partner in its own redemption. As Hugo Rahner interprets the symbol, the Incarnation

> is not some radiant epiphany in which a man appears in the full power of his manhood; it is a birth from the womb of a virgin, who, as the epitome and representative of an earth that was ready for redemption, receives into herself the coming of God: the sun of Christmas forms a union with the Christmas moon and from this conjunction, both bridal and motherly, from this supernatural *synodos,* comes the procreation of all divine life for all the days to come; that union continues its effectiveness in the baptismal birth of those who in the Church form the mystical body of Christ on earth.[29]

She may be ancillary, but the power of the ancient Moon Goddess is expressed even in patriarchal Christianity, in the transformative vessel of the baptismal font. And consciously or unconsciously, Mary drew to herself in popular piety and art the symbols and the functions of the ancient goddess: the moon at her feet and stars for her crown, as the cosmic woman of the Apocalypse had been described (Rev. 12:1), the robes of sky-blue, the rays of light extending from her hands; she is invoked, like Diana, as patroness of fertility and childbirth and charged, because of her power over the sea, with the protection of mariners.[30]

The luminous serenity of the moon in its positive phase enabled Christian thinkers and artists to portray Mary as the ultimate spiritual transformation of the feminine principle, a kind of Sophia in which all heaviness and materiality are transcended. This same luminosity and tranquillity led to the comparison between Mary and air, the pervasive, omnipresent element of the vault or vessel of the heavens. The theme appears relatively late in Western theological writing, between the 13th and 16th centuries. The groundwork had been laid much earlier, however, in traditions which brought out the air's additional dimensions of creative sustenance, nourishment and protection—mothering dimensions which are found par excellence in the divine spirit, the life-breath which brooded in the beginning over the waters.

Cicero notes (*De Natura Deorum* II.26.66) and Augustine mocks the Stoic theory that the air in its softness manifests Juno, wife of Jove. The vivifying sweetness of the atmosphere in the *locus amoenus* was a classical commonplace; Virgil speaks in his Elysium of the spirit which sustains ("*spiritus intus alit"*) the heaven and earth (*Aeneid* VI.726). In Christian terms, the *topos* was picked up in the hexameral tradition, which retold the Genesis account of the six days of creation; to Ambrose, all things in the newly created world were "sustained and nourished" by the air above.[31]

The Syrian poetry and hymns of St. Ephrem bring together the hexameral tradition with the Scriptural theme of the "ruah Jahweh," the breath of God which dwells in man. For Ephrem, the air is a major symbol of the divine grace which pervades the universe, yet leaves the human person free:

> With everything also is there mingled this air on which our breath hangeth. Though its fetter gall us not, it entereth into us and cometh forth from us, and is unto us as though it were not. The hand falls upon it and it is not felt beneath it; it flees without changing while it is in the hand; when it is taken, it lets itself not be taken. Its breath passes through bodies, things bound in it are as loose things, that turn them whithersoever they please. They come and go in the midst of it. On one Breath all depend. It beareth all without weariness; in His fulness they all dwell; and as in an empty space they abide. He is too great to be hidden in any thing. Lo! He is covered though not hidden, for with Himself He veileth Himself.[32]

For Ephrem, the air of Paradise encompasses the universe. It is also definitely feminine and maternal in relation to humanity. In his hymns on Paradise, Ephrem calls its air "a fountain of sweetness/ From which, in early life/ Adam inhaled nutriment," and the inspiration of it "was to his youth / Like the ministering breast of a mother." The Garden is "the vital breath/ Of this diseased world."[33]

Theologians were understandably more slow than poets to see the feminine dimensions of their patriarchal God, in spite of the feminine imagery of the scriptural figure of Wisdom. They were also predictably careful when the Marian analogue was proposed, to confine it to its dimensions of purity and serenity rather than creative power. But the comparison survived. In his sermon notes, Gerard Manley Hopkins pondered Catholic belief in Mary's intercession in terms which accent her luminous reflection of the source of grace:

> St. Bernard's saying, All grace given through Mary; this is a mystery. Like blue sky, which for all its richness of colour does not stain the sunlight, though smoke and red clouds do, so God's graces come to us unchanged but all through her. Moreover, she gladdens the Catholic's heaven and when she is brightest so is the sun her son: he that sees no blue sees no sun either, so with Protestants.[34]

In his poem "The Blessed Mother Compared to the Air We Breathe," the comparison comes to life, and re-creates more of Ephrem's sense of dynamic, spirit-filled motherhood. The wild, "world-mothering" air is a "needful, never spent,/ And nursing element"; it is "more than meat and drink,/ My meal at every wink," and by "life's law" his lungs must breathe it. So Mary, "merely a woman," has power beyond any goddess; she *is* mercy, as is the air, and "mantles the guilty globe," a "wild web, wondrous robe." Hopkins firmly anchors Mary in a Christian, not pagan, setting; her one work is to "let all God's glory through," to conceive Christ and so to temper the fire of the divine sun to our human weakness. But it is her *work*, not her passive presence; she is a "sapphire shot,/ Charged, steeped sky," filled with power and energy.

If images of Mary in spite of themselves persist in encroaching upon divine prerogatives and functions, and the young woman of Nazareth winds up overshadowing the Spirit who had originally overshadowed her, we can account for the tension in two not mutually exclusive ways: orthodox Christian symbolism does not adequately mediate the full range of transcendent reality and its operations among human beings; neither does the traditional Christian model of the "tamed feminine" adequately represent to humanity its experience of the possibilities of this principle on a human level. Mary the "sky goddess" is a symptom of our dissatisfaction on both counts, and our attempt to gather up the fragments into a living whole once more. Male and female are the *imago Dei*. The glory of Yahweh in Ezekiel's apocalyptic vision blazes like fire on a sapphire throne (Ezech. 1:26-28); the Spirit of Yahweh scourges the sinful race of mankind for its sins, and breathes life back into its dry and scattered bones, step by step, as a mother's womb shapes her child into being (Ezech. 37:1-10).

Sisters of a Sort

No study of Marian symbolism, however brief, can ignore the two typological themes which underlie patristic treatment of her from the beginning of her existence as a "mystical" rather than historical entity: the types of Eve and of the Church. In the freely shifting patterns of Christian typological thought, the theme of Mary as the "new Eve," mother of the living, emerges earliest of all and is maintained consistently over the centuries.

Although Paul treats Christ extensively as the second Adam, he only mentions Mary once, and then not by name, in the epistle to the Galatians (4:4). Justin Martyr introduces the parallel of Mary and Eve in the second century: Eve conceived from the serpent, and brought forth disobedience and death; Mary obeyed the message sent from God, and brought forth the Savior.[35] Irenaeus develops its consequences: Eve caused death for the whole human race; Mary becomes its rescuer, untying the knot of her first mother's disobedience.[36] Eve, says Gregory of Nyssa, bore children in pain; Mary both began her pregnancy and completed giving birth in joy.[37] Eve is proud; Mary humble. Eve seeks knowledge; Mary, faith. Eve sews garments of shame; Mary, of righteousness. Eve says no to God; Mary, yes.

Occasionally, but not often in the long line of con-
trasts, the two women regard each other directly in
sisterhood. Irenaeus in an interesting phrase calls
Mary the "advocate" or comforter of the downcast
Eve. The Syrian poet Jacob of Sarug sees Mary as a
child stretching out her hand to her "prostrate
ancestress" and raising her up.[38] One of Ephrem's
hymns pictures Mary with her infant son, rejoicing in
the redemption that has thus come to the first mother:

> Let her lift up her head that was bent low under
> the garden's shame. Let her uncover her face
> and give Thee thanks, because Thou hast taken
> away her confusion. Let her hear the voice of
> perfect peace, because her daughter has paid
> her debt.[39]

We owe these brief moments of insight to the richer
emotional content of the Syrian tradition. In the West,
Eve and Mary are almost always conveniently-posed
adversaries, and little more.

Mary did perform one definite service for Eve, by
tempering the vituperation which some of the Fathers
saw fit to hurl at her. Tertullian's words stand all too
available to those who wish to trace misogynism in the
Christian tradition:

> Do you not believe that you are [each] an Eve?
> The sentence of God on this sex of yours lives
> on even in our times and so it is necessary that
> the guilt should live on, also. You are the one

who opened the door to the Devil, you are the
one who first plucked the fruit of the forbidden
tree, you are the first who deserted the divine
law; you are the one who persuaded him whom
the Devil was not strong enough to attack. All
too easily you destroyed the image of God,
man. Because of your desert, that is, death,
even the Son of God had to die.[40]

The Virgin qualified this outrage, if only by obliging
the moralists to follow the typological arc to its other
end in her, and acknowledge that Eve's failing was
redeemable. Only the most singular and extraordinary
virtue could counterbalance what was seen as the
weight of Eve's sin, however, and so patristic treatment of Mary was pushed in spite of some reserva-
tions in the direction of a greater and greater accent
upon her holiness.

It was also moved to attribute to her those virtues
which Eve by the Genesis account seemed especially
to lack: humility, obedience, subordination to her
male partner. In the light of the gift of the Incarnation,
the Fathers could pronounce the Fall in general a
"felix culpa," or happy fault, but they addressed this
jubilant assessment to Adam, not his wife. Eve's drive
to consciousness and self-assertion was in no way to
be encouraged; she was fixed as a negative role
model, and insofar as Mary undid the damage of her
act, Mary too was fixed in opposition to the type of
the female temptress.

In the Jewish tradition, it is interesting to note,

another legendary temptress, Lilith, causes Eve to be moved to the side of the positive feminine principle. Adam's first wife, according to medieval Jewish commentators, Lilith was created by God from the dust of the earth, exactly as Adam had been. When Adam demands her obedience, and assigns her the inferior position in the sexual act, Lilith rebels, insisting on her equality, and leaves both Adam and the garden in a fit of rage. Having learned his lesson the hard way, God creates a second, more docile wife for Adam from his rib during sleep, as described in Genesis 2.

Lilith has since functioned as a symbol of unbridled female sensuality and selfishness—until a recent group of feminists put another ending on the story: Eve and Lilith meet each other, share their stories and become friends. Adam and God are both expectant and afraid of the possibilities, as the two women return to the garden together to rebuild it.[41]

There is so little of the theme of sisterhood in either Testament, actually, that patristic writers can hardly surprise us by their failure to develop it. The Book of Ruth etches a brief, moving cameo of woman's loyalty to woman in the relationship of Ruth and her mother-in-law Naomi: "Wherever you go, I will go . . . wherever you die, there I will be buried" (Ruth 1:16-17)—stubborn, undying commitment through loss and journey into strange lands. Otherwise, the male transmitters of the word of God concentrate on male/male or male/female models: the themes of brotherhood, whether positive (David and Jonathan) or negative (Jacob and Esau); parenthood (father/daughter, mother/son); and marriage. When women are shown relating to one another, it is almost always negatively, with a man's attention somehow at stake. Rachel and Leah compare and are jealous; Herodias manipulates her husband through her daughter Salome; even Martha and Mary seem to bicker over Christ. One would like to know: What was Mary's relationship with Mary Magdalen, or with the other women among the disciples—not her blood or marital ties, but her feelings, her expectations, the level of her sharing as time went on. If the question was unimaginable to the Evangelists, was the reality non-existent?

In the developing structures of the new Church, as far as we can see, sisterhood is not so much an ideal for its own sake as it is a protective sexual measure: widows whose primary relationship to a man is in the past tense can now safely minister, especially to the needs of other women, preserving the segregation of the sexes and the purity of priests—they must be old widows, however, for younger ones are still suspect (cf. 1 Timothy 5:9-15).[42] And the growing groups of virgins in the 3rd and 4th centuries were not encouraged to orient themselves to one another, but to Christ as their "spiritual bridegroom."

The relationship of Mary and Eve in patristic thought reflects commonplace notions of comparison, competition and subordination to primary male relationships, as well as the unfortunate growing belief in the virginal woman as necessarily superior to her married sister. Woman won her new acceptance in the spiritual realm, as Rosemary Ruether so succinctly puts it, at the price of despising real, physical women, sex and fecundity.[43]

And while considerable moral energy flows between the two poles of the Eve-Mary comparison in the writings of the patristic period, none flows from them into the future until a second theme is introduced: that of Mary as a type of the Church. This too is of fairly early origin, and has lasted down into our own time, finding new life in the renewal of vision expressed by Vatican II.

Ambrose is the first of the patristic writers to make this typology explicit: both Mary and the Church are virgin and mother; the mystical body of Christ was formed in Mary's womb, along with his physical body; she *is* the Church in embryo, standing at the foot of the Cross, and everything that is enacted in her will be enacted later in the Church itself.[44] Augustine develops the comparison further:

> Mary gave birth to your Head, the Church to you. For she [the Church], too, is both mother and virgin; mother through her charity, virgin through the integrity of her faith and piety. She gives birth to nations, but they are members of the One whose body and bride she is herself, and in this bears likeness to that virgin [Mary], because she, too, is the mother of unity in the many.[45]

Thus the title "Mother of the living" passes from Eve to Mary, and from Mary to the Church; the

young Christian community adopts both bridal and
maternal imagery to express its identity, and Mary
enters into another polarity, this time with an
eschatological thrust that preserves the possibilities of
lively historical development.

Mary did not, of course, give the Church its character as a feminine type. The image of the Church as
spouse of Christ goes back to Paul's vision of the
mystery symbolized by marriage (Eph. 5:32); the first
Christian commentaries on the Canticles identified the
Shulamite with the Church and the individual soul
rather than with Mary. As the bridal and maternal imagery combine in the mystical Marian tradition, they
will give rise to a certain confusion of roles; Ephrem,
the first to call Mary the bride of her own son, also
pictures her asking Christ what she is to call him,
whether son, brother, spouse or Lord.[46]

But the parallel between Mary's role as mother and
the day-to-day work of the Christian community in
bringing Christ into the world was clear, and every individual soul who participated in building up the community could be seen to participate likewise in the
work of Mary giving birth.

Mary's virginal womb thus becomes a symbol of the
baptismal font: as in her womb was engendered the
physical Christ, so at the baptismal font Christians
gain a brand-new life as children of God. It was the
same spirit, Leo the Great observed, which gave Mary
and the "fountain of baptism" the power to conceive.[47] The one exception between the two, Augustine wrote, is that Mary brought forth but one child,

while the Church is destined to mother many into salvation.[48]

For each Christian, daily growth in Christ continues the work of baptism. Hugo Rahner quotes a Cappadocian from the fourth-century circle of St. Gregory of Nazianzus, on Matthew 12:50:

> Every soul carries Christ within herself as in her womb. But if she is not transformed through a holy life, she cannot be called Christ's mother. Yet whenever you receive Christ's word within you, and let it live in your heart, and build it up with your thoughts as in the womb, then you can be called Christ's mother. Are you a just man? Behold, you have built up Christ within you. Are you a generous man? Behold, you have formed within you the image of Truth itself.[49]

Likewise, those who share their faith with the world responsibly are carrying on the maternal role; according to Gregory the Great:

> he is above all the mother of Christ, who preaches the truth; for he gives birth to our Lord, who brings him into the hearts of his hearers; and he is the mother of Christ who through his words inspires a love of our Lord in the spirit of his neighbor.[50]

Augustine is careful to state that Mary was also a member of the Christian community, as well as a type of it. The community among which she was included might look back directly to the original "Mother of the living" as its Biblical foreshadowing. In Augustine's most famous typological interpretation of the parallelism of Old and New Testaments, Mary is not even mentioned; rather, he sees the blood and water which poured forth from the pierced side of Christ on Calvary as representing the sacraments which are the essence of the Church, just as Eve, its type, was formed by God from the side of the sleeping Adam.[51]

Nevertheless, once it took hold, the explicit typological identification of Mary with the Church persisted on into the Middle Ages. When the two began to be separated again at that time, Hugo Rahner points out, it was with loss on both sides.[52] But perhaps the greater loss was on the side of the Church, for the medieval period evolved a tender human cult of the Virgin, while the Church was seen more and more as a purely juridical institution.

Unintegrated Power

Carefully controlled and integrated into the patriarchal framework of Christianity, the positive elements of the feminine principle had been acknowledged as having a certain legitimate place; in Mary, they began to be more and more enshrined in all their nobility. But the negative elements, particularly the dynamic ones, had no symbolic outlet beyond the figure of the hapless Eve. The shadowy side of the Mother-Goddess went underground, to reappear in subversive and disinherited figures like the witch.

And occasionally, in the unauthorized but irrepressible popular religious imagination, the shadow bobs up in the very person of the Blessed Virgin herself. We have seen the tentative speculation among some patristic writers about possible imperfections and even faults in Mary. But these are always faults connected with feminine weakness, corrected in due time by the instruction and guidance of her son. The full force of the dynamic negative side of the feminine is connected not with weakness but with power—the power of self-assertion, anger, active sexuality, disregard for societal conventions or rational principles of thought and behavior.

The lawlessness of the medieval Virgin, and her use of her supernatural powers to protect sinners from just punishment, might have won a less securely-situated woman swift death by burning at the stake. For she reads minds and hearts, as witches are said to do, and in her presence people find themselves thinking new and unconventional thoughts. Mary's disregard for the discipline of the Church formed an entire category of her medieval miracles, as in the case of her readiness to heap anger on a bishop who dared to take action against one of her favorite priests, ignorant and corrupt as the latter was. She will more readily forgive the nun who runs away from the cloister to her lover, even stepping in to perform the wayward sister's duties so that she will not be missed.[53]

The people, Henry Adams suggests, loved Mary precisely because she trampled on conventions.[54] Nor was she above jealousy; witness her severity with knights who deserted or neglected her for another woman.[55] She exasperated even the devils by the exercise of her arbitrary power, and challenged the judgments of the Trinity:

> Mary concentrated in herself the whole rebellion of man against fate; the whole protest against divine law; the whole contempt for human law as its outcome. . . . To her every suppliant was a universe in itself, to be judged apart, on his own merits, by his love for her—by no means on his orthodoxy, or his conventional standing in the Church, or according to his correctness in defining the nature of the Trinity.[56]

The questions Adams raised for himself on his pilgrimage to Chartres at the beginning of our century—why did Mary's cult seem to be a separate religion, why did she wield such exclusive power over rich and poor alike, why did she so exasperate the Puritans, why was the Holy Spirit not a sufficient expression of love and grace in the Protestant churches to take her place—are not dead questions as the century draws to a close. If anything, they are more alive, for we are asking again about the place of the active feminine principle within both Catholic and Protestant religions, and if place is not made for it the possibility of a separate cult is again real.

In his own way, Adams idealizes the Virgin, looking back wistfully from the viewpoint of a crumbling culture and anticipating the new "Dark Ages" with aristocratic distaste, world-weariness and self-distrust.

But the anima figure he projects is a force as well as a dream; although he identifies the feminine mind with the laws of inertia, the Virgin he describes is as dynamic as any machine on the modern horizon.[57] Besides the Mary of medieval *exempla* and miracles, even the imposing French queens from whom she took so much of her coloring seem tame—they, after all, did not have the power of eternal damnation in their arsenal of weapons.

The figure of Mary gradually accumulated power not only in the popular imagination, but in medieval theological writing as well. Here, of course, her power is directed only to conventionally positive purposes; yet unintegrated as it was with the concepts of God and Church, it led to serious distortions from the viewpoint of orthodoxy.

A certain extravagance already marked Byzantine eulogies of the Theotokos at the end of the patristic period. Germanus of Constantinople (d.733) called himself her slave, and counted upon her intercession because God obeyed her in all things as his mother.[58] The notion of her queenship was a commonplace in the East when Autpert introduced it to the West in the 8th century.[59] For John the Geometer, Mary is the radiant pole of the universe, frightening even heavenly spirits by her transcendence.[60]

In the West too, growing emphasis is placed upon her unique relation to the Trinity. God willed us, in St. Bernard's view, to have everything through her.[61] Another 12th century abbot, Godfrey of Admont, calls her mistress of the world, queen of heaven, em-

press of angels, and "unique matter of all the
sacraments."[62] By the 13th century, theological
writers are speaking of the "omnipotence of Mary,"
and Bernardine of Siena (d. 1444) remarked that she
had done more for God than God did for men[63]—a
sentence which perhaps helps to explain the feelings
of the reformers toward the Marian cult.

There are some who view the phenomenon of
courtly love, whether manifested in religious or in
secular form, as a positive step toward the maturing of
relations between the sexes and the overall growth of
human consciousness. Certainly the civilizing effect of
a value system which engenders art and song, and
channels human aggression into stylized confronta-
tions such as jousts and tourneys rather than the
perilously real game of patriarchal war, ought not to
be dismissed. But courtly love was an upper-class
pastime. The feudal social organization held the seeds
of its own decay, and the Hundred Years' War hardly
demonstrated that any lasting commitment to *gen-
tilesse* was established by the glance of "my lady's fair
gray eyes." On the religious level too, the courtly love
of the Virgin encouraged an outpouring of creative
expression, left doctrine in pieces, and the society
over which she was held to preside so regally, for the
most part unchanged. Power unused is power un-
proved.

With the revaluations of the 16th century, Mary's
role in Protestant worship was diminished to the point
of non-existence; her treatment in Catholic circles was

considerably sobered at the same time. The willfulness and imputed power of the feminine principle could still flash out, as in the practice of "slavery to Mary" in the 17th century, and in some of the Marian visions of our own time. But on the whole, even when her force was acknowledged, it was of the elementary, not the dynamic feminine character, and its effect was of the time-honored elementary kind: the preservation of the status quo. Her power did not lead to the empowerment of others. The woman who more than anyone else symbolized the nature of "the feminine" to men, usually symbolized half the story.

Doctrine and Worship

If the cult of the Virgin in general was a source of irritation to the reformers and a stumbling-block to the cause of ecumenism, the proclamation of the dogmas of the Immaculate Conception (in 1854) and the Assumption (1950) seemed to cement forever the impossiblity of reconciliation among the Christian churches.

As we have seen, belief in the first of these two doctrines developed slowly. The liturgical feast of Mary's Conception was kept in the Byzantine Church as early as the 7th century. The Eastern theologians and poets who wrote of Mary's stainless holiness were not taking a stand on the doctrinal controversy, however, for they had a vastly different concept of original sin, as general human weakness and mortality. Heir to the Augustinian formulation in terms of moral failing, the West was also heir to bitter arguments over Mary's exemption from such sin, arguments that were prolonged and exacerbated by the loyalties of religious orders to one or the other side, depending on how their favored theologian had pronounced himself. The feast of the Conception was brought to the West by those fleeing the Iconoclast persecutions of the 9th century, and had reached England before the Norman Conquest. It was introduced in Lyons, France, in the 12th century, provoking severe protest from St. Bernard despite his love for the Virgin. The Council of Basle decided to approve the doctrine in 1438, but only after the Council had been officially dissolved, so that the decree did not have binding force; the men of the Church spent four more centuries in controversy before Pius IX made his solemn definition in the mid 19th century.

The feast of the Assumption, or of Mary's "falling asleep," dates from an even earlier period. It was celebrated in the Eastern Church from perhaps the fifth or sixth century, and was introduced in Rome about 650 A.D. The idea of the Assumption had been suggested hesitantly some years earlier by the bishop Epiphanius (d. 403);[64] it was carried widely through East and West alike by apocryphal versions of the *Transitus,* or story of Mary's passing into heaven. Some of the apocryphal narratives depict Mary as summoning the Apostles to her deathbed; they witness her death and see to her burial, but after three days in the tomb her body is taken up to heaven by angels. Other versions do not include her death, or if they do, follow it with the immediate rejoining of her body and soul. Particularly in the West, Assumption iconography concentrated on an active physical ascent of the Virgin into the heavens, rather than the more typically Byzantine image of her dormition, or death-bed scene.[65] Many preachers quoted from the *Transitus,* reinforcing the popular sense of the suitability of sparing the Mother of God from physical corruption. Indeed, the concept engendered far less bitter dispute on all levels within the Church than did that of the Immaculate Conception, despite the greater length of time which intervened before its solemn proclamation by Pius XII.

Still, the two doctrines are often grouped in modern mariology, facing severe accusations about their lack of scriptural foundation and their detrimental effect on the ecumenical cause. Yet their feasts are part of a long liturgical tradition; their celebration was and is dear to the hearts of many to whom the circuitous lines of theological argument would mean little even if they could follow them. Although it is hardly the only criterion of our faith, a kind of emotional and poetic understanding will not be gainsaid. Modern Scripture scholarship has sharpened our awareness that the Biblical themes and images so freely embedded in the liturgies of the two feasts are relative to Mary only in a derivative sense—but their resonance was never a strictly factual one to begin with. A sense of the historical plenitude encompassed by Mary—the uroboros, or roundedness created by the snake biting its own tail—led liturgists to join the prophecy of the serpent's downfall in Genesis with the cosmic woman of the Apocalypse, radiantly crowned and robed, as appropriate analogues of the full working out of the Incarnation. The jubilant triumph of her faith seemed worthy of the praise given Judith ("You are the glory of Jerusalem, you are the great pride of Israel, you are the highest honor of our race"), or the beloved in the Canticles, "all beautiful, without stain."

Both feasts express symbolically perceptions which are open to varied theological expression. The Virgin Mary, human woman that she was, led the way in faith for us to God, establishing in her own person and in the son whom she bore the possibilities of human union with the transcendent. She lived the union for which we are all destined from the beginning of our lives, the union to which we will personally one day go, through whatever barrier or valley of shadow we must—or rather, the union that will come to us, not in a far-off heaven but in the meeting-ground of our hearts, if we choose to have it so. Perhaps if we stop looking at the two doctrines primarily as privileges which separate her from us, and consider their affirmation of the divine love for human nature, we will find them worth the saving work that must be done to recast them in terms more appropriate for the late 20th century.

We should note as well, whatever the political expediency or personal neurosis which was attached to her cult along the way by the men who theologized, proclaimed dogmas and constructed liturgies, through the centuries they nursed a spark of insight into woman's capacity to hear and live the divine word for herself.

To nurse an insight and to act upon it are, of course, two different things. More than one recent observer has pointed out the deplorable condition of actual women in countries where Marian devotion has been most intense. The developing irony of our time, however, lies in another paradox: that the one Christian church which kept most squarely before the eyes of history Christ's choice to be intimately affiliated with a woman, and which preserved for 20 centuries its sense of itself as the feminine recipient of transcendent love, should also be the most reluctant of all the Christian churches to consider admitting women to its ordained ministry.

The reasons for its reluctance are complex and deep-rooted, and can hardly be treated with justice in this limited space. But we cannot pass over the topic without recognizing that Mary herself has been used quite frequently as evidence for the nondemeaning nature and intent of the traditional exclusion of women from the priesthood: Surely Christ would have ordained her, the argument runs, if he had wanted to ordain any woman? Her role of humble handmaid is "the better part" for women; they betray "feminine spirituality" and the right order of things by seeking to stand in the spotlight of the altar.

Apart from the fact that we do not know what role Mary did play in the early Church, the argument raises serious questions about the vision of priesthood it implies; the more one exalts the non-ordained status lived by Mary, the more one seems to be describing her son at the same time. Far from being proper to women alone, simple presence and service were clearly two major components of Christ's own ministry and of his commission to the Twelve. That women could mediate and represent God to the rest of humanity was not an insight accepted by his country in the first century A.D. But we do make a leap in judgment by assuming that Christ intended to freeze the structure of his community forever at the level of his own historical period; this would cancel out many other developments of ecclesial life, including the Roman Curia, religious orders and mariology itself.

Behind the accusations of pride, ambition and unwarranted innovation made by those who object to the idea of women as Roman Catholic priests lies genuine concern for the integrity and continuity of the apostolic tradition. Deeper in the shadows lies ancient prejudice, and the most physical possible interpretation of what pertains to a priest. At a regional discussion of the issue, a male seminarian asked how a woman could possibly say the words of consecration—"This is my body"—with authenticity. A woman at the conference gently asked the seminarian to consider the authenticity of Mary's fashioning the body of her son from her own flesh. It was not meant as a snappy answer, though he may have experienced it as such.

Meanwhile, in view of the feminine imagery of the ecclesia, a young woman whose sense of her Church is at odds with its present structures, had her own "sexist" question: "How can all those men go around calling themselves a 'she'?"

Into the Future

Reading accounts of behind-the-scenes strategizing at the Vatican Council, one could wonder whether integrating the Council statements on Mary into the Constitution on the Church was a solution based on genuine belief in the intimate connection between ecclesiology and mariology, or rather on the hope that Mary, her embarrassingly fervent devotees and the ecumenical problem represented therein would conveniently "get lost" in the ecclesial perspective.

Be that as it may, a recent survey of Marian scholarship tells us in effect that the Council's vision has taken hold among mariologists: there has been a fall-off of interest in the themes of mediatrix and co-redemptrix, and an increase in studies of her virginity and her relation to the Church.[66] We have moved, in Rene Laurentin's view, from the ancient sense of Mary's place in the *communicantes* to a renewed balance and sense of shared fellowship with her, having passed through unbalanced exaltation of her to a place above the Church and through the extreme diminishment of the Reformation.[67]

Two points, however, must be noted. The Mary with whom we are sharing "fellowship" is still a Mary imaged through the eyes of men, or 49% of the People of God. Neither mariology nor ecclesiology can yet claim to have benefited substantially from the vision and self-understanding of the female half of the race, still less from the dynamic dialogue between the sexes that must await the expression of this understanding. It seems self-evident that the measure of the Church's willingness to call forth this expression and to allow it a full share in the renewal and reshaping of the ecclesia will be the true measure of its sincerity in restoring Mary to her "proper place" among us.

But it cannot be a simple matter of expecting women to speak for "the feminine," echoing all the anima projections of the ages from the pulpit once they are permitted to enter it. Human beings are not archetypes, still less the "half-archetype" that men made of the Virgin in idealizing her. At most we mediate to each other some of the possibilities and tendencies of the never completely known or understood symbolic principles of "the masculine" or "the feminine," and we do this best when we do it spontaneously and unself-consciously. The woman who is trying to be feminine and the man who is trying to be masculine are both liable to trip over their own feet, to be acting a part rather than expressing real being.

Equally sad, they are cutting themselves off from areas of unknown power and potential within themselves—the animus which is in a woman, the anima which is in a man (rather than projected outside of himself, onto a figure like Mary).

If we are to be true to our times, perhaps it is not so much a matter of "restoring" Mary to her ancient place as it is of allowing her to take the place which has been opened up for her by the insights of the age in which we live: the place of a fully human person who continues to grow even now in knowledge and love of a dynamic God, and vital sympathy and commitment to the community which is becoming the full measure of her son.

Similarly with the Church: if "Father" is a good but incomplete title for God, it seems we must also look into the possibility that "Mother" is a good but incomplete expression of the Christian community, especially as it moves into the future, seeking to relate on an adult level within itself and with the rest of the human race. "Mothering" is not a total expression of feminine potential, just as feminine potential is not the only dimension of ecclesial being.

Herein lies the richness of an honest and close exchange between mariology and ecclesiology: as new models of the Church's being develop and interact with one another, they interact also with our sense of the person who stood absolutely open to such growth from the first moments of the Church's existence. The community founded by her son seeks now to incor-

porate varied and conflicting images of itself; in Avery
Dulles' terms, it feels the pull of the very different ec-
clesiologies of church as institution, as community,
sacramental mystery, herald or proclaimer of the
word, and servant to the world. As it works out its
identity, it can look to her who was similarly called to
reconcile within herself the pieces of a puzzle that
didn't always seem to fit, and to set in motion a process whose end she could not see.

For the community is also the sum of the human
beings who comprise it, and like each of them has its
own "task of the self" to complete. The model of
Mary reassures us that the mystery of personal being
is at the center of this corporate entity, testing and being tested by it. Different things may be asked of us—
but in the end, no more than what was asked of her,
and with the same faith, the same baptism, the same
Spirit to help us respond.

Conclusion

Being a character in someone else's dream is tricky business, as Tweedledum and Tweedledee teach Alice in the world behind the looking glass. She is "only a sort of thing" in the Red King's dream, they tell her. If he wakes up, she will be nowhere; she will go out "bang! just like a candle."

Alice protests loudly that she is real, and starts to cry. But since they have defined her as a thing in a dream, even her tears can't count as real tears. Neither can she wake the Red King up and prove them wrong: being *in* the dream, she can't also be outside of it.

The only practical solution to this logical impasse is to walk away from those whose definition set it up—which she does.

The more women orient themselves to their position as real, autonomous beings in a real world, the shakier seems to them the existence of anyone who chooses to continue living mainly in someone else's dream, and the more tenuous becomes a figure like the mystical Mary, held up by so many men as a role model for women.

If the male half of the race were ever to take back their anima projections, and integrate their own capacity for the contemplative, the receptive, and the emotional side of being, would the figure of the Virgin go out, "just like a candle"?

It will, if we define her as essentially created by a patriarchal dream, or if we hold her historical person to be so irretrievably lost that it cannot anchor the intuitions and hopes of any age. There is clearly some evidence for both these viewpoints, and neither one in itself would mean the end of Christianity. On the positive side, if the candle did go out, the energy given to keeping it aflame might be redirected to outlets which more effectively foster personal maturity and collective interaction.

On the other hand, it might not. Energy can get lost without symbols to direct it. Few of either sex have spent much time before Mary's altar in recent years, yet we can hardly claim unparalleled personal integration or collective dynamism in the present Church.

Those who suppose the answer is in lighting bigger and better candles to her, and bringing back May-crownings and Marian praises after Mass, deserve the lack of response they are probably going to get from many segments of the People of God. To underestimate the degree of resistance the old symbols will encounter is to underestimate the profound contempt for the elementary feminine embedded at this point in all of our psyches, and the profound fear that such a Marian piety actually presided over evil and did not challenge it. The mentality of Vatican II rested very much on the sense that the Church had become too passive, too comfortable with the *status quo,* too "feminine." One senses also behind the energy and aggressiveness of the American bishops' current campaign against abortion their determination to avoid the inertia and lack of leadership in German Catholicism at the time of the Nazi genocide.[1]

Looking back now, it is possible to speculate that the reforms of Vatican II were themselves implemented in a too one-sidedly "masculine" way—by decree, like lightning from the skies, bolstered by theological reasoning more than by emotional commitment and understanding. The Council Fathers seemed to be aware that traditional forms of Marian piety were not going to be viable for many in the renewed Church; they had no more idea of how to re-create that piety for our own time than they did of how to "tell the folks back home" what they had come to see in the conciliar sessions. No group (particularly a single-sexed group) can do everything.

Still, in its own way the impetus of the Council gave many a keener and more vital awareness of the richness of their faith. It helped women religious, in particular, to come in touch with their powers of decision and action, and to take control over their own lives as adults, integrating the animus factor into their development—though not, needless to say, without pain and doubt. A genuinely revivified Marian piety for our time would have to take all that has happened in the lives of women since the Council into account. Perhaps it is the women of the present who must re-dream the Virgin, and extend her mystical reality on into the church of the future.

To have any permanent meaning, this would have

to happen in a way that is intrinsically connected with our experience of the modern church and world, and of ourselves, and at the same time a way that avoids wrenching her from the foundation of her historical self.

The last thing that is needed is another case of projection or of wish-fulfillment. We would have to ask of the re-symbolized Mary things we are also prepared to ask of ourselves: honesty, integrity, mature personhood, responsible relation to people and to the God toward whom we are moving. Nor could a truly potent symbol emerge from the intellectual experimentation of a few; it is not a matter of designing the "new Mary" in our heads and then unleashing her upon the world like a Madison Avenue ad campaign. If a Mary is going to be re-created by women, then it stands to reason that she be re-created in a specifically feminine way—slowly, quietly, out of the substance of our already-present diffuse awareness of her and of all that the mystical Christ has added to her being. To paraphrase T. S Eliot, we know more than she—and she is part of what we know. What we need to do is bring our knowledge to the surface.

Another part of our knowledge is the contemporary expansion of the concept of womanhood itself. The feminist movement of recent years has taught many a new sense of respect for themselves, as well as a new sense of sisterhood, and a broader understanding of the dimensions of motherhood. A revived Mary-symbol would somehow have to express all these, as ideals which are in the process of becoming realities.

For myth and life feed and re-create one another, adding coherence and clarity to direct experiential awareness.

In fact, the "new woman" (who may actually be as old as Susan B. Anthony or the Grimke sisters or Aphra Behn) is already functioning as such a myth in the secular sphere, and many of her qualities would not be out of place in a truly religious realm: courage and integrity of conscience; passionate commitment to human rights; concern for the conditions in which most women live, not simply those of her own class or race; willingness to sacrifice for the values which she has chosen, rather than those mandated to her by her culture and the men in her life.

We know women are capable of these things because we have seen them lived and passed on, even through the squint-eyed vision of traditional secular history. Unfortunately, though religious history may put an occasional phenomenon up into the niche—Catherine of Siena, Joan of Arc, Teresa of Avila—these seem very far from us now, women whose brief flash of genius was swiftly swallowed up in the institutional darkness, and who never had more than limited effect on the conditions of women in their own time, let alone on the permanent structures of church and society. (It took 489 years to canonize Joan of Arc; 28 for Therese of Lisieux, the "Little Flower"; 48 for Maria Goretti.)

For the last century and a half, at any rate, secular women have been living out the charism of feminine activity and involvement in the world, and we may be grateful that it has come down to us through them. But it is not enough. Because of the absence of parallel figures on the religious horizon, other qualities have not yet been strongly integrated in our minds with the notion of womanhood: an active relationship with God; religious prophecy inspired enough to be taken seriously in its own time, if not its own country; theological insight; the use of power as stewardship (consider the concept of "stewardess"); the sacred goodness of female sexuality.

Our vision has not been broadened to include faith in the presence of the divine in the material, the ordinary, the events of daily life; the dialogue of man and woman as imaging the life of the godhead; or religious acceptance of full personhood and wholeness as holiness. On the contrary, we have been given ample precedent on the religious level to identify the qualities of strength, honesty and prophetic confrontation when exercised by women as sin, error or neurotic maladjustment. Many a nun dressed in quite decent, even dowdy street clothing has been made to feel a devilish cross between Eve, Lilith and Jezabel, and more than one married woman trying desperately to hold her marriage and her emotional stability together has come away from the confessional convinced she was damned to hell. A woman who aspires to leadership is accused of ambition and lack of humility; one who tries to express a vision different from that of male authority is undermining the Church and not giving "our men" the support they need to do a hard job.

"No one has ever loved an adventurous woman as they have loved adventurous men," Anais Nin writes in her diary. "This struggle to live by my own truth is so difficult, so wearing. I am like the adventurer who leaves all those he loves, and returns with his arms full of gold; and then they are happy and they forget how they tried to keep this adventurer from exploring, from his voyage and his search."[2] Catholic women of the post-Vatican II era have experienced the first part of this process; the official Church is still at best postponing judgment on the quality of the gold. Sometimes we are led to doubt it ourselves. Our personal credo has not been designed from scratch, like Anais Nin's, but every element in it has borne the sharp and steady inspection of radical questioning. We live by a truth that is more than personal, that carries with it the support of prayer, Scripture study and communal discernment—but it is a truth which has not been fully shared with the rest of the ecclesia which means so much to us.

This is the point at which the re-symbolizing of Mary appears as empowerment to continue the journey, and also to "share the gold" which we have already found. Though she is most at home in the communion of saints, Mary is not just another saint; fully human, she stands as no other human being has done at the borderline of the immanent and the transcendent. Insofar as she stood "for us" before God, she stands "for us" to us. She can help us to tell one another what we have found in ourselves, what we can bring transparently before the Most High for acceptance and ratification. A good symbol catches up and gathers more reality than ideas or words can formulate; Marian symbolism not only gathers up reality, but brings it into the sphere of eternal value.

Can such a Mary underwrite the modern woman's search for a self and her respect for the self that she finds? For the symbol of the Virgin has often been used by the Church to undermine, not strengthen, the female self. If Marian piety does not break with the extreme self-hating and self-emptying school of ascetical thought, we may pray indeed that it does fail, for it would then be feeding the vein of masochistic self-disgust which our culture has bred into so many of its women.

The misogynism of Tertullian and his kind was at least overt; the misogynism of our time is packaged attractively and humorously, and therefore more lethally—in every friendly but empty-headed female TV character who hearkens to the voice of the male expert on toilet bowl cleansers or drapes herself over the new-model car as its automatic accessory; in every school guidance counselor or teacher who assumes marriage is the female student's only goal, and guides her course choices accordingly; in the flood-tide of cosmetic advertising which plays on woman's fears of aging or failure to measure up to the current image of the beautiful; in every film or drama which shows an unmarried woman as neurotic and unfulfilled; in the male newscaster who advises women to enjoy rape since there is nothing else they can do about it.

Woman after woman has looked into the mirror of our culture and found herself invisible, or at best a charming shell, all surface and no content, and even the surface wearing down as she watches. She does not know who she is as a person, and the language of traditional asceticism serves her not at all. How can you empty what is already an empty space? The profound concept of kenosis meets defeat on its own grounds; one can speak of "emptying oneself" of morbid self-doubt, or vain fears and anxieties—but these are inverted expressions of emptiness to begin with. The double negative is no longer even stylistically elegant; psychologically it sets up a contorted approach to the problem, and spiritually, Christ warned about the mindset which specializes in house-cleaning: the last state is indeed worse than the first (Matt. 12:43-45).

There is, as we have seen, room enough for pain and sacrifice in the task of the self. But the sacrifice of one who knows she is moving toward a goal which she desires, one who freely names as holy (*sacer facere*) realities which she chooses to relinquish on her journey, is a far cry from the one who continually and compulsively denies herself because she feels, somehow, that she is unworthy, or that pain and poverty are in themselves equivalent to holiness. Can Mary enter into a spirituality which values life, and life to the full?

For reasons discussed earlier, women have difficulty establishing the ego identity from which they can make spiritual choices. Often they are led to beg for a

"room of one's own," in Virginia Woolf's phrase—
physical and psychic space within which to con-
template and work out the beginnings of a personal
voice. When the lack of such a basic integrity is felt,
commitments already made come under the pressure
of a new duty, which demands re-adjustments. One
role, or two or—not uncommonly, twenty—added up
will not by themselves give woman the key to her
identity. So Ibsen's Nora slams her famous door. "I
would give my life for my children," says a similar
character in Kate Chopin's *The Awakening*, "but I
wouldn't give myself."[3] She has reached clarity about
her values, but not about how to express them in
practice, and in the hostile environment of the nine-
teenth century society which does not understand
her, the conflict leads to suicide.

Twentieth-century attitudes are not always more
supportive. Other women speak of experiencing a
loss of control, a purposelessness, a sense of moving
hypnotically through life: "What frightened me most
was the sense of drift," writes Adrienne Rich:

> the sense of being pulled along on a current
> which called itself my destiny, but in which I
> seemed to be losing touch with whoever I had
> been, with the girl who had experienced her
> own will and energy almost ecstatically at times,
> walking around a city or riding a train at night or
> typing in a student room. I was writing very little,
> partly from fatigue, that female fatigue of
> suppressed anger and the loss of contact with her

> own being; partly from the discontinuity of
> female life with its attention to small chores, er-
> rands, work that others constantly undo, small
> children's constant needs.[4]

She manages to pull herself and her world together by
adopting a new honesty in her poetry, learning to express and give a shape to her anger as well as her
love. It is not unwillingness to take responsibility that
had been sidetracking her, but inability to unite the
"energy of creation" and the "energy of relation"
when the world defined her purely by the latter—
"woman's role."

There are no doubt a goodly number of husbands,
bishops, pastors, and business executives who mutter
to one another that women are going through a stage,
and if it hadn't been for this fad of an identity crisis
started by a few articulate trouble-makers, their wives
would be happily hovering over the kitchen stove,
their convents full of cheerful and obedient teaching
sisters, their secretaries still working twice as hard for
half the pay. They do not seem to grasp that any
movement which overcomes women's profound dis-
trust of one another and dislike of uprooting the *status
quo* has its roots not in a fad, but in a basic need and
hunger of the human person for meaning.

Contrary to the fears of the male half of the race,
and the euphoric optimism of some early participants
in the woman's movement about the power of sisterhood, it is also a task, and not an automatic response.
Women are as capable as men of jealousy, competi-

tiveness, stereotyping, pettiness, vanity and power struggles—though *not* more so. We bit the apple too. The historic separation of women from each other has wrought consequences which are going to have to be worked out in patient dialogue and mutual sharing among women of different classes, races and religions; within and among religious communities, between sisters and "lay" women (new terminology needed here!).

We also need a Mary-symbol which can underwrite this sharing, not by imposing one arbitrary model which all women must live up to, but by endorsing the interaction of many models, their ability to cooperate, support and challenge one another in their growth. Only if various models feel themselves to be of equal dignity and worth can there ever be the creation of a new bonding of women in which diversity is seen as an asset, not a flaw, and focus on the peculiar problems or satisfactions of our own "primary" community or state in life does not blind us to the reality of those in another. "O Mary," Anne Sexton prays, "open your eyelids."[5] Women have gifts to give one another; we are our "sister's keeper" as much as our brother's, and the two are not mutually exclusive.

Perhaps most urgently of all, we need a religious symbol which can clarify and express the full truth of motherhood in the modern age: a symbol which fosters respect for the woman who feels called to be a mother, and also for the woman who does not, and which reduces no woman in the course of her choice to either sheer body or sheer spirit. Can the Madonna mediate the possibilities of generativity, in fact, on a wider scale for both sexes, the possibility and often the desirability of giving more life to what is already born, rather than beginning a new one? Or the mothering implicit in laying the groundwork for the world of the future, without possessively demanding to see the harvest of what we sow right now, or in our immediate progeny? To put it another way, can she— and we—endorse Christ's reflections on his dialogue with the Samaritan woman at the well, his sense of the long, slow process of bearing spiritual life, a process which outlasted even his lifetime, though some ripe fruit fell into his hands in a single conversation. One sows, another reaps. Can she call forth—and we come up with—the tough faith required for the long haul, in which we reap the toil of others, and sow our own for later harvesting?

While it is hard for us to envision the traditional Madonna slamming a door, or announcing to Gabriel that she will give her life for her son but not herself, we are faced in the Gospel with a Christ who does affirm woman's right to her own identity, and places more value on her spiritual well-being than on her physical childbearing. The Christ who told Martha in effect to get out of the kitchen and attend to the one important thing can surely co-exist with a Mary who re-orders her priorities and upsets the balance of the conventional social expectations of the sexes. But can the Church?

Probably only when it has learned to live with real women who have kept up Mary's habit of saying *fiat,* and trying to be faithful to the resulting partnership with the transcendent in their own lives.

For that is where the new image of Mary is going to be realized—not on a fresco or a statue to the side of the main altar, or on holy cards that look like the Bionic Woman rather than the Mona Lisa—but in the members of the ecclesia. In those utopian days to come, men as well as women will prove the capacity of humanity to bring body and spirit, thought and feeling, contemplation and action, love and justice, self and others into unity in the light of the divine. In the meantime, we share what we have: abiding faith that this unity can happen, and that we can help to bring it about.

How far away is the millennium? It is a good deal further, certainly, than the first female Little Leaguer or altar girl, or the first woman Supreme Court justice, or the first Catholic woman priest or bishop. But the reasons for both sexes working to achieve it are getting more compelling by the day. The present system is not working. The rising rates of divorce, rape, child abuse, the decay of our cities, the plight of the aged, the impotence of our penal system, literally shout this in our ears.

Men as well as women suffer. Adrienne Rich points to the deep pessimism and fatalistic grief in the poetry of current male writers, and wonders if it isn't the masculine side of the price we are paying for patri-

archy. But if we choose, she feels, the suffering can
be birth-pains:

> just as woman is becoming her own midwife,
> creating herself anew, so man will have to learn
> to gestate and give birth to his own subjectivity—
> something he has frequently wanted woman to
> do for him. We can go on trying to talk to each
> other, we can sometimes help each other,
> poetry and fiction can show us what the other is
> going through; but women can no longer be
> primarily mothers and muses for men: we have
> our own work cut out for us.[6]

The work of repairing the divisions and confronting
the evasions within ourselves and our own sex is
humbling work, not arrogant narcissism blind to
human need and pain. We are always more genuinely humbled by the new than the old, for we have not
been able to build up defenses and we have no laurels
to rest on; we cut a comic figure, not a noble one, to
most eyes as we search out new paths.

But the Church itself will never complete the task of
its self until its individual women members have made
headway in reconciling their own androgynous capabilities in a truly active, confident, mature
womanhood, and been accepted fully for who they
have named themselves to be. Until this happens, the
ecclesia will fail to bear witness to our age that God
does find female creation good, and has other things
to talk about with it besides birth control and abortion.

And it will also fail to bear witness that God finds male creation good in itself, that man need not prove himself by brutal domination of the weak or ruthless acquisition of material goods; for man's attempt to raise himself up as master of a group he can dominate for his own ends is the most glaring symptom of his own lack of confidence in himself and his worth. A Church which is infected with this dis-ease can hardly challenge it in others.

In the meantime, if they are lucky, women discover the transcendent on their own, and keep on the journey toward it. An "awful rowing," Anne Sexton calls her search, though God and she have a splendid game of poker in the end, and neither loses; blisters and all, like Sarah of old she matches "his" untamable, gut-driven laughter and delight in their relationship.[7]

It is this knowledge—and this laughter—which women must offer to one another today, while we work and wait for its integration within the institutional life and worship of the Church. The transcendent has always had more in mind for us than human culture has been able to envision; powered now by no "voices" nor by a paternally comforting supreme father figure, but by our own inner awareness of loving and being loved, we have the strength to keep on rowing.

Mary the woman who lived open to the transcendent, bringing herself into the deepest connection with it and relating freely and unself-consciously to others, is for us a comfort on the way, not because she answered the needs of the ages for a mother figure, or led us to the lost side of God, but because she was a real, historical person who brought her self to the world of her time. The limits of her humanity did not lead her to dodge responsibility; the limits of her womanhood did not keep her bound to conventional thought or action. To put her back in her historical period is to gain a deeper assurance from her than any Great Earth Mother could ever give us, because, although we know so few details, we know that a real human person bore Christ in faith, and so, that we can do it too.

We also believe that as we do, we add to the dimensions of her life and mission in the mystical Christ. According to Augustine, we didn't know who Eve was until Mary came; if so, then it can be said that we didn't know who Mary was until we became, and our carrying out of our mission in the twentieth century as the People of God leads to a fuller apprehension of her identity.

We are not gods and goddesses, but fallible human beings. Neither sex is exempt from the search, and neither sex can use a projected Mary as a weapon against the other as we struggle to shape the future Church. Perhaps for our time her best title is not "mother," but "sister in faith," not one who directs or defines our way, but one who reminds us of the resources we carry with us as we go. We want her with us on the journey, despite the bitterness and skepticism of some who see her as the ultimate patriarchal weapon: this is but to concede that men can keep on coming between women and dividing them, that conversion and transformation cannot reach back into the past and undo it, that the names which patriarchy gave must stick.

We want her with us because no one else testifies in quite the same way to the scars of patriarchy and the power of a woman to come up smiling in spite of them; no one else stood so well by our parents in the hour of their death, and by their parents and grandparents before them; no one else holds our past as she holds it, and looks expectantly into the future, hinting that perhaps we really haven't seen anything yet, compared with the fullness that is to come.

Appendix

A Weighing of Conscience for Christian Women Today

Weighing, measuring, sifting, pondering, is "feminine" work. The first task assigned to Psyche in her drive toward light and love is to sort a huge and hopelessly confused jumble of seeds, fruits, and grains, and to do it before nightfall. She is overwhelmed by the task, but friendly ants come to her aid, and one by one, carry each lentil, bean or barley grain to its proper pile.

The Gospel counsels us that sorting wheat from chaff is the work of a lifetime, and premature judgment can be destructive. But it also invites us to a sincere weighing of the larger moral quality of our words and deeds—unlike the Pharisees, who strain off gnats but miss camels, tithe herbs but omit the weightier demands of justice, mercy and good faith (Matt. 23:23-24). Slowly, gently, but decisively, we must discriminate and put right the confused welter of dispositions, drives, ingrained patterns of thought and action, by which we contribute to the sin of the world, the burden of Christ.

1. Have I said yes when I should have said no? (To really unreasonable claims on my energy; to tasks

which I did not have the time or ability to fulfill in justice; to those which another person or group would grow and profit from doing if only given the opportunity; because I could not admit my own limitations or tolerate being seen as less than generous?)

2. Have I said no when I should have said yes? (To a role which challenged and offered me real responsibility; to a call which required me to sacrifice security or comfortable routine; to a position or stand which seemed unfashionable; because I could not admit a mistake; out of sheer perversity; out of cynicism; out of habit?)

3. Have I spoken when I should have been silent? (When someone needed time and space to work out what I spoke glibly or patronizingly; when I wanted to prove something that is either realized from within or not at all; when I have been speaking too much and my head has run ahead of my heart; when I should have been listening, to God or another person?)

4. Have I been silent when I should have spoken? (When I saw or heard injustice, but didn't want to disturb anyone or hurt feelings; when a person or group needed my vision but I just didn't feel like getting involved; when I was in need and ashamed to admit it; when I should have written to a) the White House, b) my Congressman/woman, c) the editor, d) the Chancery, e) my pastor, or f) any other person of authority who didn't see all that he/she should?)

5. Have I stayed in touch with reality? (God; myself; the people close to me; my neighborhood / parish / city / country / world? Have I failed to accept and deal with my own anger? my sexuality? Seen these gifts as intrinsically less than good? Have I kept growing, and been open to new ideas and discoveries?)

6. Have I taken from any person or group their rightful power to define themselves? (Judged them without knowing them; presumed I knew what was best for them; manipulated them to serve my needs; allowed political, economic or social oppression to go unchallenged; oppressed others with my unreal expectations of them, or my lack of any expectations?)

7. Do I believe and act on the belief that women are made in the image of God? that men are too? (Do I put women down as a general rule, excepting myself; put women down, including myself; put men down with no exceptions; do I listen equally well when a man or a woman is talking to me; when a sister or a laywoman is talking to me?)

8. Have I used a) the gifts, b) the head, c) the heart God gave me? Am I grateful for them?

Footnotes

INTRODUCTION

[1] *Constitution on the Church,* Chapter 8.

[2] Cf. Mary Daly, *Beyond God the Father* (Boston: Beacon Press, 1973), and Margaret Farley, "New Patterns of Relationship," *Theological Studies,* 36 (1975), 627-646.

[3] Doris Lessing, *The Golden Notebook* (New York: Bantam Books, 1973), pp. 471-72.

[4] Daly, pp. 74-75.

CHAPTER ONE

[1] Cf. Edward Schillebeeckx, *Mary, Mother of the Redemption* (New York: Sheed and Ward, 1964), p. 5; Max Thurian, *Mary, Mother of All Christians* (New York: Herder and Herder, 1964), p. 25.

[2] *The Reed of God* (New York: Sheed and Ward, 1944), p. xii. Cf. also Raymond Brown, *Biblical Reflections on Crises Facing the Church* (New York: Paulist Press, 1975), pp. 106-7.

[3] Erich Neumann, *The Origins and History of Consciousness* (Princeton: Princeton University Press, 1970), pp. 33-38.

[4] Rix Weaver, *The Old Wise Woman: A Study of Active Imagination* (New York: G. P. Putnam's Sons, 1973), p. 115.

[5] Irene Claremont de Castillejo, *Knowing Woman* (New York: Harper and Row, 1973), pp. 14-26.

[6] Erich Neumann, *Amor and Psyche: the Psychic Development of the Feminine* (New York: Pantheon Books, 1956), pp. 112-14.

[7] Leonard Swidler, *Women in Judaism: the Status of Women in Formative Judaism* (Metuchen, N.J.: Scarecrow Press, 1976), pp. 54-55.

[8] J. Massyngberde Ford, "Biblical Guidelines to Marian Devotion," *Review for Religious*, 35 (1976), 363-64.

[9] Swidler, pp. 114-25.

[10] Cf. Rachel Adler, "Tum'ah and Toharah: Ends and Beginnings," *Response*, No. 18 (1973), pp. 117-24.

[11] Paula E. Hyman, "The Other Half: Women in the Jewish Tradition," *Response*, p. 69, and Rachel Adler, "The Jew Who Wasn't There: Halacha and the Jewish Woman," *Response*, p. 80.

[12] Jacob Benno, "The Jewish Woman in the Bible," *The Jewish Library*, III (London: Soncino Press, 1970), p. 1.

[13] Thurian, p. 42.

[14] Ford, p. 361.

[15] Hilda Graef, *Mary: A History of Doctrine and Devotion*, I (New York: Sheed and Ward, 1963), 215-21.

[16] Ibid., pp. 298-302.

[17] Hilda Graef, *The Devotion to Our Lady* (New York: Hawthorn Books, 1963), p. 35.

[18] John Macquarrie, *Christian Unity and Christian Diversity* (Philadelphia: Westminster Press, 1975), pp. 93-94.

[19] Schillebeeckx, p. 25.

[20] Graef, *Mary: A History*, I, 183, 187-89 ff.

[21] Ibid., pp. 40-46, 75-76.

[22] Ibid., pp. 50-51.

[23] John McHugh, *The Mother of Jesus in the New Testament* (New York: Doubleday and Company, 1975), p. 132.

[24] George Maloney, *Mary, the Womb of God* (Denville, N.J.: Dimension Books, 1976), p. 22.

[25] Francoise Mallet-Joris, *A Letter to Myself* (New York: Farrar, Straus & Co., 1964), p. 17.

[26] Ann Belford Ulanov, *The Feminine in Jungian Psychology and in Christian Theology* (Evanston: Northwestern University Press, 1971), pp. 171-72.

[27] Ibid., p. 160.

[28] Ibid., p. 177.

[29] Ibid., p. 187.

[30] Ibid., p. 191.

[31] Cf. Esther Harding, *Women's Mysteries, Ancient and Modern* (New York: Bantam Books, 1973), pp. 167-69.

[32] Graef, I, 78-79.

[33] Harding, p. 147.

[34] Ibid., pp. 170-82.

[35] Evelyn Hinz, *The Mirror and the Garden* (New York: Harcourt, Brace Jovanovich, 1973), p. 111.

[36] McHugh, pp. 65-67.

[37] Ibid., pp. 167-69.

[38] Ford, pp. 367-69.

[39] The amount of influence the Essenes had upon Christ is variously estimated; cf. A. Dupont-Sommer, *The Essene Writings from Qumran* (Cleveland: Meridian Books, 1962), pp. 368-78; John M. Allegro, *The Dead Sea Scrolls and the Origins of Christianity* (New York: Criterion Books, 1957), pp. 155-62.

[40] Cf. J. Massyngberde Ford, "Mary's Virginitas Post-Partum and Jewish Law," *Biblica*, 54 (1973), 269-72.

[41] Marie-Louise von Franz, *The Problem of the Puer Aeternus* (New York: Spring Publications, 1970), VII, 10.

[42] M. Esther Harding, *The Way of All Women* (New York: Harper and Row, 1975), p. 239.

[43] Cf. Maloney, pp. 14-15.

[44] Neumann, *Amor and Psyche*, pp. 85-86.

[45] Weaver, pp. 57-58.

[46] Thurian, pp. 117-44. Cf. Brown, pp. 96-101.

[47] *Dictionary of the Bible* (Milwaukee: Bruce Publishing Company, 1965), p. 552.

CHAPTER TWO

[1] Marie-Louise von Franz, *Problems of the Feminine in Fairy Tales* (New York: Spring Publications, 1970), pp. 39-41.

[2] *On Holy Virginity*, 3, quoted by Hugo Rahner, *Our Lady and the Church* (New York: Pantheon Books, 1961), p. 43.

[3] Sermon I on the Nativity, quoted by Rahner, p. 43.

[4] Sidney Callahan, *The Magnificat: the Prayer of Mary* (New York: Seabury Press, 1975), pp. 33-36.

[5] Jean Galot, *Mary in the Gospel* (Westminster, Md.: Newman Press, 1965), pp. 210-11.

[6] Brown, pp. 96-101.

[7] Elizabeth Carroll, "Women and Ministry," *Theological Studies* 36 (1975), 670-73.

[8] And businesswomen as well; cf. Lydia, "seller of purple" (Acts 16:14).

[9] George Tavard, *Women in Christian Tradition* (Notre Dame: University of Notre Dame Press, 1973), pp. 4-12.

[10] Neumann, *Amor and Psyche*, pp. 112-14.

[11] von Franz, *The Feminine in Fairy Tales*, p. 159.

[12] de Castillejo, p. 133.

[13] Maloney, p. 82.

[14] Thurian, pp. 13-19; McHugh (pp. 50-52) is less certain that the parallel in Luke is deliberate.

[15] Cf. Piet Van Boxel, "The God of Rebekah," *SIDIC: Journal of the service international de documentation judéo-chrétienne*, IX (1976), 14-18.

[16] Cf. the section on the Lar by Marie-Louise von Franz, *A Psychological Interpretation of the Golden Ass of Apulius* (New York: Spring Publications, 1970), I, 9-12.

[17] Cf. David Daube, *The New Testament and Rabbinic Judaism* (London, 1956), pp. 27-51, and Ford, *Biblica,* pp. 271-72.

[18] Professor Ford points out the relevance of this passage in *Review for Religious,* p. 371.

[19] Cf. McHugh, pp. 50-51.

[20] Ibid., pp. 48-49.

[21] Ibid., p. 78.

[22] von Franz, *The Feminine in Fairy Tales*, pp. 33-34.

[23] Virgil's retelling of the myth in his Fourth Eclogue was frequently "baptized" by Christian commentaries applying it to the Virgin Mother of Christ. Cf. Marjorie Hope Nicolson, *The Breaking of the Circle* (New York: Columbia University Press, 1962), pp. 91-96.

[24] Ford, *Biblica,* pp. 269-71.

[25] Ford, *Review for Religious,* p. 370.

[26] Cf. Brown, pp. 101-104.
[27] von Franz, *The Feminine in Fairy Tales*, pp. 33-34.
[28] Ulanov, p. 296.
[29] Ibid., p. 297.
[30] Ibid., p. 301.

CHAPTER THREE

[1] Carl Jung, "A Psychological Approach to the Trinity," *Psychology and Religion: West and East*, Vol. XI of *Collected Works* (Princeton: Princeton University Press, 1969), pp. 170-71.
[2] Anne Sexton, "Consorting with Angels," *Live or Die* (Boston: Houghton Mifflin Company, 1966), pp. 20-21.
[3] von Franz, *The Feminine in Fairy Tales*, p. 21.
[4] Erich Neumann, *The Great Mother* (Princeton: Princeton University Press, 1972), pp. 42-43.
[5] Ibid., pp. 44-54.
[6] Rene Laurentin, *The Question of Mary* (Techny, Illinois: Divine Word Publications, 1964), pp. 160-66.
[7] Graef, I, 48.
[8] Ibid., p. 237.
[9] Ibid., p. 175.
[10] Ibid., pp. 193-94.
[11] Maloney, op. cit.
[12] Graef, I, 102.
[13] Ibid., p. 111.
[14] Ibid., p. 113.
[15] Thurian, pp. 42-55.
[16] Trans. by Roy J. Deferrari, *Saint Ambrose: Theological and Dogmatic Works* (Washington, D.C.: Catholic University of America Press, 1963), p. 181 ff.
[17] Graef, I, 195.
[18] Graef, *The Devotion to Our Lady*, p. 57.
[19] Trans. by Paul F. Palmer, *Mary in the Documents of the Church* (Westminster, Md.: Newman Press, 1952), p. 51.
[20] Graef, I, 93.

[21] Cf. Margaret B. Freeman, *The Unicorn Tapestries* (New York: E. P. Dutton, 1976), pp. 50-51, 136.

[22] Stanley Stewart, *The Enclosed Garden: the Tradition and the Image* (Madison: University of Wisconsin Press, 1966), pp. 43-44.

[23] Graef, I, pp. 60, 65-66.

[24] Ibid., pp. 237-39.

[25] Cf. Joseph Campbell, *The Mythic Image* (Princeton: Princeton University Press, 1974), pp. 58-64, and Marina Warner, *Alone of All Her Sex: the Myth and the Cult of the Virgin Mary* (New York: Alfred A. Knopf, 1976), p. 47.

[26] Neumann, *The Great Mother,* p. 55.

[27] Ulanov, pp. 160-62.

[28] Neumann, *The Great Mother,* pp. 56-58.

[29] Hugo Rahner, *Greek Myths and Christian Mystery* (New York: Harper and Row, 1963), p. 156.

[30] Cf. Warner, pp. 255-69.

[31] *Hexameron,* V. 1, *Saint Ambrose: Hexameron, Paradise, and Cain and Abel,* trans. John J. Savage (New York: Fathers of the Church, 1961), p. 159.

[32] Ephrem, "Rhythms upon the Faith," *Select Works of S. Ephrem the Syrian,* trans. J. B. Morris (Oxford: John Henry Parker, 1847), pp. 122-23.

[33] "Hymns on Paradise," *Select Metrical Hymns and Homilies of Ephraem Syrus,* trans. Henry Burgess (London: Blackader, 1853), pp. 113, 117.

[34] *Sermons and Devotional Writings of Gerard Manley Hopkins,* ed. Christopher Devlin (London: Oxford University Press, 1959), p. 336.

[35] Graef, I, 37-38.

[36] Ibid., pp. 39-40.

[17] Ibid., p. 67.

[38] Ibid., p. 120.

[39] Palmer, p. 19.

[40] Tertullian, *The Apparel of Women,* trans. Edwin A. Quain, *Tertullian: Disciplinary, Moral and Ascetical Works* (New York: Fathers of the Church, 1959), pp. 117-18. Cf. Rosemary Rad-